Better Homes and Gardens

WATER GARDENS

POOLS, STREAMS & FOUNTAINS

Meredith® Books
Des Moines, Iowa

Better Homes and Gardens® Water Gardens: Pools, Streams & Fountains
Editor: Denny Schrock
Contributing Writer: Barbara P. Lawton
Copy Chief: Terri Fredrickson
Publishing Operations Manager: Karen Schirm
Senior Editor, Asset and Information Manager: Phillip Morgan
Edit and Design Production Coordinator: Mary Lee Gavin
Editorial Assistant: Kathleen Stevens
Book Production Managers: Pam Kvitne, Marjorie J. Schenkelberg,
    Rick von Holdt, Mark Weaver
Contributing Copy Editor: Amanda Knief
Contributing Map Illustrator: Jana Fothergill
Technical Proofreaders: Ray Rothenberger, Bill Uber
Contributing Proofreaders: Karen Fraley, Stephanie Petersen,
    Missy Peterson
Photographers: Scott Little, Blaine Moats
Contributing Photo Researcher: Susan Ferguson
Other Contributors: Janet Anderson, Kate Carter Frederick,
    Mary Irene Swartz
Indexer: Ellen Sherron

**Additional Editorial Contributions from
    Art Rep Services**
Director: Chip Nadeau
Designer: lk Design

Meredith® Books
Executive Director, Editorial: Gregory H. Kayko
Executive Director, Design: Matt Strelecki
Managing Editor: Amy Tincher-Durik
Executive Director/Group Manager: Benjamin W. Allen
Senior Associate Design Director: Tom Wegner
Marketing Product Manager: Isaac Petersen

Publisher and Editor in Chief: James D. Blume
Editorial Director: Linda Raglan Cunningham
Executive Director, New Business Development: Todd M. Davis
Executive Director, Sales: Ken Zagor
Director, Operations: George A. Susral
Director, Production: Douglas M. Johnston
Director, Marketing: Amy Nichols
Business Director: Jim Leonard

Vice President and General Manager: Douglas J. Guendel

Better Homes and Gardens® Magazine
Editor in Cheif: Karol DeWulf Nickell
Deputy Editor, Gardens and Outdoor Living: Elvin McDonald

Meredith Publishing Group
President: Jack Griffin
Executive Vice President: Bob Mate

Meredith Corporation
Chairman and Chief Executive Officer: William T. Kerr
President and Chief Operating Officer: Stephen M. Lacy

In Memoriam: E. T. Meredith III (1933-2003)

Thanks to
Adams Aquatics, Aquascape Designs, Inc., Beckett
    Water Gardening, Liquid Landscape Designers,
    Van Ness Water Gardens

Contributing Photographers
(Photographers credited may retain copyright ©
    to the listed photographs.)
L = Left, R = Right, C = Center, B = Bottom,
    T = Top

Heather Angel/Natural Visions: 229L; **Roger
Bannerman/Wisconsin Department of Natural
Resources:** 127T; **Brian Bevon/Ardea.com:** 228,
**The British Museum/Topham-HIP/The Image
Works:** 6; **Bob Brudd:** 232, 233; **Gay Bumgarner/
Positive Images:** 55B; **Rob Cardillo:** 41, 142; **Eric
Crichton/Garden Picture Library:** 194L; **Geoff
Dann/Garden Picture Library:** 192R; **R. Todd
Davis:** 183L, 191R, 201B; **Alan & Linda Detrick:**
193L, 201T, 203R, 218R; **Catriona Tudor Erler:** 38,
58B, 75T; **Mary Evans Picture Library:** 7; **Derek
Fell:** 12, 13B, 202, 205R, 237B, 238R; **Max Gibbs/
Oxford Scientific:** 235L; **John Glover/Garden
Picture Library:** 198L, 201C; **John Glover/Positive
Images:** 165B; **Jerry Harpur:** 30B (Penelope
Hobhouse), 33, 51B (Little & Lewis), 111B, 137B;
Marcus Harpur: 133, 161, 193R; **Lynne Harrison:**
50 (Suzanne Edison Design), 186L, 192L, 197R, 221B;
Sunniva Harte/Garden Picture Library: 237T;
Doug Hetherington: 55T, 77B, 81, 94, 97, 234;
Saxon Holt: 29R, 59, 68, 71B, 160B, 173B, 183R;
Jerry Howard/Positive Images: 35; **Bill Johnson:**
199, 200; **Nick Johnson/Positive Images:** 148R;
Dency Kane: 179R; **Lynne Karlin:** 204R; **Art
Kowalsky/Alamy Images:** 8; **Andrew Lawson:** 21B
(Simon Shire), 40T, 69T, 79B (Paul Bangay), 132,
137T, 160T (Sidergarden.com), 163 (G. Robb), 178
(Roy Day & Steve Hickling), 189R, 196R, 210R,
Janet Loughrey: 196L; **Hanson Man:** 224, 225L,
226, 227; **Ivan Massar/Positive Images:** 203L;
Marilynn McAra: 190R, 215L, 220; **Medio Images/
SuperStock Inc.:** 9; **Clive Nichols:** 60, 139T (Keeyla
Meadows); **Jerry Pavia:** 10, 21T, 25B, 39L, 122,
125T, 129, 135, 139B, 162T, 189L, 191L, 198R, 213R,
214, 221T, 236B, 239T; **Gary Rogers/Garden
Picture Library:** 223; **Konrad Schmidt:** 235R;
J. S. Sira/Garden Picture Library: 182L, 197L;
Greg Speichert: 204L, 207L; **Keith Sutton:** 229R;
Michael Thompson: 4, 18, 40B, 47B, 82, 131, 148L,
180T, 182R, 185L, 186R, 188, 205L, 207R, 209L,
213L, 222; **Pat Wadecki:** 219R; **Alex
Zatschkovitsch/Flora Graphics:** 108, 206, 210L,
211R, 215R, 216, 217, 218L, 219R

On the cover: Photographer: **Clive Nichols**;
Landscape Designer: Paul Dyer

TABLE OF CONTENTS

CHAPTER
HIGHLIGHTS

This chapter provides inspiring glimpses

into the history of water gardening.

Study the wide variety of water features

you can add to your own landscape—

pools, fountains, waterfalls, rivulets,

rain gardens, bog gardens, dry creeks,

container water gardens, and indoor

water gardens. The possibilities are

nearly endless.

INSPIRATION FOR WATER GARDENS

The sight of a beautiful garden pool, the sound of a waterfall, the touch of a water-cooled breeze–these are some of the sensual treasures that water features can bring to your landscape. You can create a backyard oasis that has the power to transform the trials and tensions of the everyday world into patience and serenity.

Water is an inspiring element that adds new dimensions to even the most modest garden. Water is calm yet alive, provides subtle reflections as well as insights into transparent depths, and serves up a sense of well-being that is hard to match in other garden features.

From the following pages, you will learn both ancient and modern traditions of water features. Before putting your water feature plans on paper, shift your imagination into the descriptions of these water gardens so that they can inspire your own magical water feature. Also, visit as many water gardens and water features as you can. Make a few notes as to what you like best–then you will be ready to begin planning your own personal water garden.

EGYPTIAN

Ancient gardens are part of today's gardening traditions and have often served as inspiration for planning modern water features. It appears that from the earliest times, people used imagination and muscle to make surroundings more beautiful and more suitable for day-to-day life. Clearly, for those earlier people as for us, a garden pool often served to cool the spirit as well as the body.

While no relics of early Egyptian water gardens remain, hieroglyphics, paintings, and other artifacts found in ancient tombs depict water gardens. The earliest planned water gardens have been documented as early as 2800 BCE. Although we don't know how or when the lotus arrived in those early gardens, we do know that the lotus served an important role in early Egyptian art, legends, and myths.

From ancient records, it's apparent that the Egyptians created their gardens within the walls that surrounded their homes. These formal gardens reflected the angularity of the walls, and often consisted of rectangular fish pools amid rows and beds of ornamental plants and fruit trees. Modern gardeners should consider including both artwork and small fruit trees in their water garden plans. Place trees far enough away from the water garden so that falling leaves and fruit do not litter the pond.

▶ This mural fragment from the British Museum depicts a formal, rectangular Egyptian pool stocked with fish, ducks, and lotuses. Date palms and fruit trees surround the pool.

MIDDLE EASTERN

Nebuchadnezzar II created the Hanging Gardens of Babylon, one of the Seven Wonders of the Ancient World. During his reign, Persians and Syrians had formal gardens that symbolized paradise, defying the hot, arid land of the Fertile Crescent. These formal walled gardens featured pools and irrigation canals.

The gardens that Nebuchadnezzar built for his wife went far beyond the other gardens of those times. His wife pined for the mountains, meadows, and streams of her home, so he created rooftop and terraced gardens on an artificial mountain. Fountains cooled the gardens. Streams, demonstrating engineering and irrigation expertise, gurgled from higher sources along terraces and slopes.

Water from the Euphrates River was carried to the top terrace by an elaborate system of buckets, pumps, and pulleys. Slaves were the source of power. The elegance, architectural majesty, and lush collections of well-watered plants made the Hanging Gardens worthy of the Wonder of the World title. Modern water gardens, using electricity to pump water, also can create water gardens with several levels.

◄ Early walled gardens of the Middle East featured formal pools and fountains said to represent paradise. These oases provided cool relief from the hot, arid climate. This mural depicts Nebuchadnezzar surveying some of his gardens.

ITALIAN

Centuries ago, wealthy Romans built summer retreats in Tivoli in the Apennine Hills of northern Italy. Hadrian's Villa, built in the 2nd century AD, remains a place where gardeners can enthuse over wonderful waterworks. The Romans enjoyed gardens built in association with their public baths. Here they could stroll and contemplate the serene surroundings.

Villa d'Este, a noteworthy 16th-century palace dedicated to water features, has fountains of all sizes, some so large that you can walk inside them. Villa d'Este even has a water feature called the Organ Fountain—the organ's

pipes, hidden under the water, play music. There are stairways with rivulets and waterfalls descending from one beautiful spot to another. Sculptured figures made into spouting fountains represent allegories.

Villa Medici in Rome is another elaborate 16th-century garden. Some features in Villa Medici are reminiscent of Babylon's Hanging Gardens. The hilly terrain in northern Italy made construction easier since gravity could be factored into the water feature designs. Today, gardeners who have property with a slope might consider developing terraced water gardens with streams and waterfalls.

▼ **Fountains and waterfalls at several levels create a dramatic effect at Villa d'Este palace.**

MOORISH

▲ Spouting fountains echo the arches of the shady adobe arcades surrounding this courtyard garden filled with blooming flowers and lush foliage at the Alhambra.

The Alhambra is a fortress, a palace, and a small city in Granada, Spain, originally constructed by Muslims. Although some of the Alhambra's excavated relics date to the 9th century, the significant portions of this magnificent monument trace from the Moorish occupation to the reign of Carlos V, from the 13th to the 16th century. Fruit trees, water, and shade are the primary characteristics of Moorish gardens. The Moghuls of 17th– and 18th–century India built similar gardens, the best known being the Taj Mahal in Agra.

Ornate tiles frame the fountains and pools of the Alhambra gardens, which comprise courtyards within cool arcades. Visitors note little channels of running water everywhere. The courtyard and surrounding arcade of the Court of the Lions focus on a twelve-sided marble fountain that rests on the backs of twelve lions. Water rises, then spills from the basin to the mouths of the lions. From there, the water descends to the courtyard rivulets.

The Muslims drew their inspiration from desert oases as well as from the ancient paradise gardens of Persia. Today's gardeners might seek spouting animal or fish fountains to incorporate in their designs.

JAPANESE

Japanese gardens are idealized interpretations of the natural landscape. Manicured evergreens, shrubs, moss, stone, water, and dry streambeds contribute to the soul of Japanese gardens. Water is a major element in Japanese gardens, and may be represented by streams, waterfalls, pools, or a lake. Water also may be suggested by dry streams and by carefully raked pebble beds surrounding boulders that hint at islands in an ocean. Water may be represented by such features as a stone basin into which water drips from a slender bamboo spout or a deer frightener, or *shishi-odoshi* , a length of bamboo that fills with water and then makes a clacking noise as it empties into a stream or basin.

Water brings stillness and peace to those who visit Japanese gardens. Miniature pools, ponds, and streams are ideal settings for plantings of irises and other water-loving plants. They are perfect for brightly colored carp known as koi. Stones and rocks that have been polished by ocean waves are often chosen as special features of Japanese gardens because they resemble islands, ships, or animals. Stones and their reflections add to the mystery and reverence of nature in these gardens.

Each segment of a Japanese garden is carefully designed and chosen to create the overall effect of peace and harmony. Individual stones and rocks offer symbolic importance. Sand may be used along the edge of a pond as a beach or shoreline. The grain size as well as the color and texture of the sand is important in creating a harmonious mix of elements.

Home gardeners can easily adapt features of Japanese gardens to their own water features. Boulders, pebbles formed into beaches, sculpted plants, and simple bamboo fountains can serve the backyard garden well.

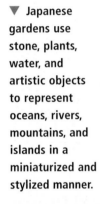

▼ Japanese gardens use stone, plants, water, and artistic objects to represent oceans, rivers, mountains, and islands in a miniaturized and stylized manner.

▲ Stepping-stones set in crushed rock lead to a traditional offset bridge inviting visitors to enter this Japanese garden.

▶ A deer frightener or *shishi-odoshi* is both ornamental and useful as it is designed to frighten deer away with its motion and clacking noise.

CHINESE

▲ Strangely eroded limestone by the shore of the water feature represents mountains by oceans or lakes in this classical Chinese garden.

Classical Chinese gardens are noted for containing one or more pools of water as well as for pavilions, arched bridges, and bright flowers. White walls surround Chinese gardens; the walls are often pierced by fanciful doorways such as the traditional moon gate. The four important elements of a Chinese garden are water, rocks, plants, and architecture. For more than 2,500 years, landscape design has been a major force in Chinese culture. The ultimate goal of Chinese gardens is to help people achieve spiritual harmony with the universe. Japanese gardens trace their heritage back to ancient Chinese gardens.

The Chinese term for landscape is *shan shui,* which literally means "mountains and water." The Chinese carefully select strange rocks and boulders of limestone that have been dented and pierced by water erosion over millions of years. These symbolize mountains by the water. The water calms the hard negative aspects of the tortuous rocks. Lively streams of water may be lined with stones so that they resemble mountain gorges.

Chinese gardens symbolize living organisms. Rocks serve as the skeleton, water as the blood, and plants as the clothing. In this traditional symbolism, various constructions–bridges, pavilions, walls, gateways, mosaics–represent human influence on nature. The overall motif of Chinese gardens is to bring people into an ideal relationship with nature, with the universe, in a balance between heaven and earth.

The traditional bridge over the water feature in Chinese gardens offers yet another place for contemplation, for inspiration, or for simply looking down into the water and allowing it to calm and soothe the spirit. Although the aim of Chinese gardens is to be spiritually uplifting, these gardens also served as settings for family gatherings, for parties, and as places for people to meet and talk.

Today's gardeners can find inspiration in elements of Chinese gardens. The watercourses, pools, gateways, and bridges can be adapted to modern water gardens.

◀ Plants often play a secondary or supporting role to rocks and water as an element in Chinese gardens.

▶ A traditional bridge accented by *tai hu,* or upright stones, along the water's edge offers a place to contemplate or meet with a friend.

EUROPEAN AND AMERICAN

Much of the water garden inspiration in North America comes from Europe. In gardening as in other fields, new styles do not erase the old ones. Rather, the new reinterprets what came before. Monastery gardens of the Middle Ages likely were inspired by early Persian gardens. Arcades and cloistered walkways surrounded gardens. Gardens were divided into four areas for growing medicinal plants and herbs, vegetables, fruits, and flowers. A fountain or a well stood prominently in the center of the garden.

During the Renaissance in Italy, extensively landscaped villas replaced the fortified castles of previous times. The grounds were inspired by Roman gardens.

By the 17th century, France became the queen of garden design as grand châteaux were created. Their designs derived from the Italian Renaissance period were formal, symmetrical gardens, which were intimidating in their grandeur. The object was to provide the impression of unlimited wealth and limitless landscaping. Hedges and trees defined alleys, avenues, and paths. Fountains and statuary punctuated the intersections and ends of these pathways. The French, because of their comparatively flat land, could not employ gravity as an important partner in water gardens as the Italians of hilly northern Italy did. Thus French water features emphasized grand scale and fountains to compensate for lack of change in elevation.

▼ **Romanticism gave rise to naturalized scenes with water features enhanced by massed plantings of shrubs, trees, and flowering plants, shown here in this large private American estate garden.**

During the late 18th century, romanticism became the leading theme of gardens. Emphasis on interpreting and idealizing the natural scene led to a new kind of landscape design. The great landscape architects of England, such as Capability Brown, replaced garden symmetry and geometric beds with sweeping vistas of lakes, ponds, and rivers in settings of meadows and fields adorned with shrubbery and copses of trees. The effect was one of natural scenes that were only slightly under human control.

▲ These classical columns bring to mind the formality of early European gardens while the fountain made in the shape of a gunnera leaf and asymmetrical plantings lend a casual air to the setting.

The romantic style spread from England throughout Europe and then to the New World. Thomas Jefferson adapted the style at his Monticello estate. America's first great landscape architect, Frederick Law Olmstead, spread romanticism from Central Park in New York City to the Biltmore Estate in North Carolina and beyond. Central Park is known and loved for its grand vistas with lawns, trees, and shrubs setting off the magnificent lake, ponds and pools, plus imaginative fountains and picturesque bridges.

▶ This unusual garden waterfall combines a dramatic one-story waterfall with a casual garden and a hint of humor.

EUROPEAN AND AMERICAN (CONTINUED)

◄ **This spectacular small-scale garden offers wide pathways leading to an intimate setting by a well-planted garden pool.**

Private and public gardens of the early 21st century have more water features than ever before. Many locales have garden tours sponsored by garden clubs and other organizations. These offer opportunities to get into gardens of private homes and see water features that are normally unavailable to most of us.

Public gardens and parks often have wonderful water features that bear studying. Most residents of the United States live within a day's drive of public gardens worthy of a visit. In New York City, there are the Brooklyn Botanic Garden and New York Botanical Garden. Outside of Philadelphia is Longwood Gardens. The Biltmore Estate in North Carolina is a grand garden. Florida offers Leu Gardens and Disney World in Orlando. The middle of the country can boast of Missouri Botanical Garden and Chicago Botanic Garden. The West Coast has Golden Gate Park and the wonderful gardens of Portland, Oregon. These are but a few of the many interesting places to study water gardens.

Tour the water gardens near you and when you are traveling to get helpful insights to designing and building your own water features. Don't forget to include the wild and wonderful places in national and state parks where streams, waterfalls, ponds, and bogs may inspire a backyard oasis.

▲ Unique water features such as these stacked stone basins can inspire similar ideas for including water in your garden. Change water frequently to prevent mosquitoes from hatching in the shallow basin.

◀ A containerized water garden featuring the bold maroon foliage of cannas, large-leafed lotuses, and flowing parrot's feather enhances the edge of a bricked terrace.

POOLS AND PONDS

Rigid liners are available in a number of shapes that serve well as basic formal water features. Formal pools are based upon uniform shapes and symmetry. Ovals, circles, rectangles, and squares lend themselves to formal design. Rigid pools generally range in size from 3×4 feet to about 8×9 feet. Formal pools usually have an even depth of water. An easy way to achieve formality is to first choose and install a symmetrical rigid pool or pond. (Remember that if your home and garden are informal in design, then a formal pool is probably not for you.) Surround the pool with formal materials such as bricks, paving blocks, or cut stone. These materials should be square, rectangular, or round, in keeping with the formal design. Carefully plan in-ground and containerized

plantings so that they enhance and underline the formality of this type of pool.

Rigid pools for informal water features are based upon free-form shapes lacking in symmetry. Irregular shapes imitate the forms found in nature. Additions of irregularly shaped rocks, boulders, and driftwood make this kind of water feature more naturalistic. The coping or edging for informal rigid pools also should be free form. Small rounded stones go well with this style. Unstructured plantings will emphasize the informality of the water feature. Plantings in the beds and borders of an informal pool should be irregular, not geometrical. Include odd numbers of each plant, rather than balanced symmetrical plantings such as those found in formal gardens.

Garden pools or ponds constructed with flexible liners offer more opportunities for unique designs than do rigid pools. Your choices of size and designs for lined pools are limited only by your lot size, budget, and imagination. Whether you develop an informal pool design to go with a natural-looking landscape or a formal one that would blend well with the geometric appearance and clean lines of a terrace or patio, flexible liners can provide long-lasting containment for your pool or pond.

Reflecting pools can create an effect, reflect a work of art, or give the impression of expanded space. They can convert an entrance area or courtyard from ordinary to magical. Place a reflecting pool where there are garden or landscape features worthy of reflection.

◄ **The sinuous edge of this kidney-shape rigid-form pool is echoed by the rounded stones that frame it and separate the water feature from the patio proper.**

◄ This round formal pool, built with a flexible liner and featuring statuary, is a handsome focal point for the patio.

▼ This formal pool combines well with classic columns united by trelliswork, a pergola, and tree roses.

Reflecting pools have a minimum water depth of 6 inches. You should not notice the pool bottom when it is filled. Night lighting increases the desired effect of a reflecting pool. Be sure that this type of pool is situated so that people do not walk into it by mistake. Build it where a wall or fence provides a backdrop. Surround it with appropriate plantings and accessorize with compatible seating.

One- or two-level pools constructed above ground are logical designs for patios. The framework may be constructed of bricks, paving stones, or wood since it will be lined with a flexible material. Square or rectangular aboveground pools are easier to construct,

although it is possible to build a round or oval raised pool of brick. An advantage of a raised pool is that less excavation is required. If there are two levels, a waterfall can link the two pools providing an impression of continuity and serenity. The materials used in construction should blend well with the existing paving of the patio or terrace as well as with the adjoining home.

If you're lucky enough to have a brook on your property, consider constructing an earthen dam that can create a pond. A skilled heavy equipment operator can complete moving the earth and contouring the surface in a day or two. The natural edges of the new pond should

▼ **Waterfalls add sound and movement to this multilevel pool, increasing attractiveness of the outdoor living spaces.**

be gentle and smooth. They will provide the perfect setting for beautiful marginal plants. The existing brook may provide enough oxygen in its water to make the pond a balanced environment for fish as well as aquatic plants.

▶ This small dammed-up natural pond with its rustic furniture for outdoor relaxation is a delightful solution to home entertaining.

▼ This raised pool with its ornamental fountain is a lovely addition to the patio. Miniature water lilies and other water plants add to its appeal. In addition, its smooth coping offers added seating.

FOUNTAINS

▲ This classic figure of a child holding a water jug is a popular fountain for home garden pools.

A great variety of fountains are available for home water features. Fountains add marvelous sound to the garden. The sound may be entertaining, serene, or it may serve as white noise to muffle traffic or other neighborhood distractions. In addition, a fountain can serve as a focal point in the garden, inviting one to relax and contemplate. It can double as a water feature and as a work of art. A fountain should look attractive even when it is not running. The surroundings of a fountain are important. Decide what the position of the fountain will be in relationship to the rest of the garden. In most

◄ This large urn makes a handsome fountain for a small pool. It is attractive even when the water is not running.

cases you'll want the fountain to stand out as the center of attention, but it should blend with other elements of the garden. When space is limited, wall fountains are a good option.

Take time to study the many choices available for fountains in home gardens today. Most are equipped with tubing ready to attach to pumps. Some come already set up with their own pump.

Traditional spitting fish, frogs, and turtles may be made of cast-concrete or durable lightweight polyresins. These statuary animal fountains sit at the edge of a water feature and nicely circulate the water to keep it fresh while not disturbing it very much— an important factor if you want to grow floating water plants.

An Oriental feature is the bamboo pump, designed to look like ones that trickle water effectively into basins of Japanese gardens. Some fountains look like old-fashioned lever-handled pumps for wells and others resemble kitchen sinks from years gone by.

Statues of children, of women holding urns or pitchers, and of other figures can be fitted as fountains. Fountain prices range from under $100 to many thousands of dollars depending on quality and size.

▶ **Developments for water features include fancy fountainheads that create unusual effects and patterns such as this bell-shape fountain.**

FOUNTAINS (CONTINUED)

Today's fountains offer many spray patterns and sequences of patterns resulting in elaborate and fascinating sprays. You may use one or several fountains in a garden pool. A single jet is ideal for a round pool while an extended oblong pool is better served by several evenly spaced fountains along its length. Consider including lighting to make the fountain even more attractive—a fountain when illuminated at night adds an exotic dimension to the garden.

Keep the fountain jet at a height of no more than half the radius of a pool to avoid spray drifting out of the pond. The height and spread of spray varies, depending on the specific fountain nozzle. The spray shapes range from cones to bursting star patterns to fleur-de-lis. You can find water-bell jets, water-tulip jets, and two- and three-tier jets as well as whirling sprays and double domes. There also are arching fountains and ring fountains. Many allow you to change patterns at will, offering the chance to match a mood simply by swapping one fountain jet for another on the fountain tube.

◀ **Imagination knows no bounds as you can see from these fountains fashioned from girders. How well they add to the modern appeal of this water feature.**

▶ With the water garden pumps and other hardware available today, you can fashion your own ornamental fountain, perhaps something like this whimsical garden watering can.

Simple inexpensive fountains that work with a reservoir are safe, small, and a good do-it-yourself project for those less experienced. Sink a bucket or other container in the ground, and fill it with water. Place a small submersible pump at the bottom and attach a small jet through hardware cloth that you put over the top of the container. Cover the hardware cloth with small stones to disguise the mechanics of the fountain.

◀ Crane fountains lend an Oriental flavor to this beautiful water garden with its attractive water plants.

WATERFALLS

Water flowing over a drop in level creates soothing sounds in a water garden and adds movement to the scene. Depending on its flow and pattern, a waterfall can gurgle or roar, trickle or splash. Choose your waterfall to fit into the design, pattern, and general mood of your garden. You can develop a waterfall for a garden pool even if the ground has no slope to it. One way is to use the earth that has been excavated from the pool to build the necessary change in grade. Another way is to use rocks or paving stones to create a rise at the back of a garden pool. A slope does not have to be large or steep to create an effective waterfall. In either case, the back of the pool should be shielded from view, hidden by a wall, fence, or evergreen planting. Provide space between the fence and the pool for a footpath for easy pond maintenance access.

Prefabricated waterfalls can easily be installed on natural or constructed slopes. Most are made of fiberglass or plastic and consist of several tiers. You can also purchase prefabricated cascades, series waterfalls, and connecting pools. One unit called a streamlet is used in series to create a cascading stream.

▶ **Imaginative use of building materials for a waterfall provides a personal signature for this artistic water feature of tile troughs.**

◀ Waterfalls come in many shapes and styles. Water sheets smoothly over the lip of this waterfall.

▼ Rough rocks form the bed of this tumbling waterfall. The multiple cascades evoke the essence of a mountain stream.

WATERFALLS (CONTINUED)

▼ This split-stream waterfall illustrates another way to create a beautiful water feature. The flowing water forms an island of perennials.

The other way to construct waterfalls is to excavate the water channel and use flexible liner to create the watercourse. The lip of the waterfall can be flat rocks or paving stones. Line the bed of the stream with flat stones or pebbles. When you conceal the edges of the flexible liner beneath rocks, soil, and plants, the end result is quite natural.

Create pondless waterfalls in much the same way as the reservoir fountains described on page 25. Pump water from the buried reservoir at the bottom to the top of the waterfall. Water then flows over the edge of the waterfall, and back into the hidden reservoir.

The lip of a waterfall is called a spill stone. The characteristics of this stone determine the characteristics of the waterfall itself. If the stone's edge is slick and smooth, water courses over it as a sheet, with no interruptions. If the spill stone is jagged, water flows over it in divided streamlets. Tune the waterfall by notching or otherwise changing the shape of the spill stone. You can also adjust a waterfall by altering the volume of water passing over it or by altering the catch basin at the bottom of the waterfall. If the basin is deep, the sound and effect will be quite different from a shallow, sloped water course that flows smoothly into the catch basin.

▲ Water cascades smoothly over this series of waterfalls. The sound this water feature makes must be soft and soothing.

◄ Creative use of rocks stacked in a stairstep manner results in a waterfall with formal flair.

RIVULETS, RILLS & RUNNELS

Rills are small brooks. Natural rills occur during heavy rains when water cuts into the soil. Rivulets also are small brooks and streams. Runnels are narrow channels for water. Rills and rivulets often occur on major watersheds where the vegetative cover has been stripped away. In land management, rills, rivulets, and runnels are bad news. But, they are good terms in water gardening. In water features, when rills, rivulets, and runnels are mentioned, they amount to the same thing. They are small brooklets or channels that carry water attractively from one place to another. While rills have been around since ancient times, they were notably ignored until Victorian times when rills and rivulets were added to geometric bedding designs.

Today's gardeners are rediscovering rills, rivulets, and runnels, using them decoratively in conjunction with other water features. Rills safely bring a water feature closer to living

▲ **This formal rill extending from a small waterfall features smooth, rounded river rocks in the base of its channel.**

▼ **This rill meanders through a shaded setting, leading to a garden pool.**

▲ This attractive rivulet with its banks of ledge rock is constructed but looks as natural as if it were on a wooded hillside.

areas. Small children can play with shallow water in a rill without the dangers associated with larger or deeper water features.

Include a rill in the construction of a paved patio by leaving a channel between the stones, then diverting water from a nearby water feature. This works especially well when there is a slight slope to the patio or terrace and the water feature consists of two pools with the upper unit at about the same level as the patio. The rill or runnel, powered by gravity, diverts from the upper level, and follows the channel down to the edge of the patio where it falls off into the lower unit.

▲ A natural-looking rivulet tumbles handsomely between and around rocks and boulders, creating a delightful combination of sight and sound.

RIVULETS, RILLS & RUNNELS (CONTINUED)

▲ **This formal runnel begins in a limestone-edged pool with umbrella palms, flows through matching channels of black stones, and ends in a catch basin.**

Rills are attractive water features for rock gardens, especially those constructed to resemble a scene from mountainous regions. Rock garden rills carry water from a basin at a high point of the garden along a channel among the rocks down to a small pool at the base of the slope. The water makes a striking contrast to the severity of rocks and stones.

A rill can imitate a feeder streamlet into a garden pond. Place a decorative water basin at the highest part of the water garden— it need only be built a few inches above the pool surface. The water will trickle down the sinuous channel to the pool. A plus of this water feature is that the water is constantly oxygenated as it flows in the rill, making ecological balance easier to establish and maintain.

A rill and the decorative water basin from which it flows undoubtedly will attract wild birds. Accessible, shallow water in a place with protection from predators is a magnet for many favorite songbirds, especially during hot, dry spells. In this way, a rill attracts the type of wildlife you want to welcome to your garden in addition to creating a lovely addition to the pool scene.

Rills, rivulets, and runnels are valuable in yet another way. If you use a rill to carry water from an upper decorative basin to a pool below, the rill will not roil or agitate the water of the pool. Since many floating water plants and most pond fish do not thrive in water that is too actively moving, a rill can benefit them by moving water in a more quiet way than fountains and waterfalls.

▲ **A formal runnel flows from an equally formal pool with fountains, creating an atmosphere of serenity and peace.**

RAIN GARDENS

Storm water specialists in Maryland were the first to develop rain gardens, also known as bioretention systems, to alleviate watershed erosion problems. These consultants realized that America's original ecosystems were perfect rain gardens. When rain fell, it filtered slowly through the plants and soils of forests, meadows, and wetlands. This resulted in unpolluted, clear, and clean streams and rivers.

Rain gardens represent a gardening concept designed to catch and clean runoff water in an attractive way. Rain gardens are replacing eroding watersheds, in not only private gardens, but also arboreta, parking lots, housing developments, and other erodible areas throughout the country.

▼ Daylilies, pink-flowered hibiscus, cannas, and zebra grass combine in this poorly drained site to make an attractive rain garden.

Rain gardens are making such a difference in erosion-prone areas that the U.S. Environmental Protection Agency (EPA) is giving grants to groups willing to heal eroded land and degraded streams. The EPA estimates that an average city block is responsible for nine times the water runoff as an equal area of woodland. Further, the agency estimates that suburban properties with their extensive lawns are responsible for approximately half of all artificial pollutants such as fertilizers, pesticides, salts, oil, grease, heavy metals, and animal waste. Small wonder that the EPA is encouraging homeowners to develop rain gardens.

Rain gardens are plantings that have been carefully designed to capture water from permeable and semipermeable surfaces—gutters, driveways, patios, and lawns—and allow it to seep slowly into the soil. Creating a rain garden prevents runoff and resulting erosion, preventing further pollution of waterways. Rain gardens also help replenish moisture deep in soils, helping to recharge aquifers. Developers of rain gardens treat rain as a valuable asset, not just another waste product.

▲ Rain gardens are excellent solutions for capturing runoff and preventing erosion, allowing excess water to seep slowly into the soil.

▼ The rain garden shown at the top of this page appears here in its spring stage, accompanied by spring-blooming bulbs.

Rain gardens replace the small wetlands that used to occur naturally before widespread development destroyed them. These natural rain gardens had lots of vegetation—trees, shrubs, herbaceous plants—and spongy organic matter that would absorb the rainwater and let it slowly seep into the soil.

In its simplest form, a rain garden is a shallow depression where rain runoff first collects, then is slowly released. The depression should not be so deep that mosquitoes can breed and standing water will drown plants. To avoid water damage to a house's foundation, place the rain garden no closer than 10 feet from the house or other building.

Site a rain garden where water runoff is prevalent. Look for low places where water naturally gathers after a deluge. Drainage areas from gutter downspouts are typical sites for rain gardens. Swales and areas at the base of slopes or hills also are likely sites. Parking areas and driveways typically have a lot of runoff, and offer rain garden sites at their lower ends where runoff is greatest.

◄ **Water-loving astilbes, hostas, and bald cypress trap the run-off from the downspout of this house.**

Rainwater can be transported from downspouts or driveways by gutter pipe or French drains (water channels filled with pebbles or gravel under the soil surface). The water flows to a shallow basin, no more than a foot or so deep. That is the foundation of a rain garden. Install a patch of gravel or pebbles at the entrance to the basin to baffle and slow the water so that it can sink into the ground. Fill the center of the basin with a mix of soil, organic matter, sand, and/or gravel to encourage the water to quickly percolate into the subsoil. Mulch the rain garden with organic matter to reduce weeds.

Observe the rain garden over several seasons to determine which parts are constantly moist and which are wet only occasionally. Those conditions will suggest what plants to use in the different parts of the garden. Plants such as rush *(Juncus)*, pickerel weed *(Pontaderia cordata)*, and thalia *(Thalia dealbata)* will thrive in the moist spots while plants such as sweet flag *(Acorus)*, New England aster *(Aster novae-angliae)*, and common rose mallow *(Hibiscus moscheutos)* will grow well in spots that dry out.

▶ **Sweet flag is a good choice for a rain garden that remains moist through the entire growing season. Its variegated foliage adds a dramatic vertical accent to gardens.**

BOG GARDENS

A bog garden can be a natural adjunct to an informal garden pool or stand by itself. In a bog the soil remains constantly wet, even soggy, throughout the year. Many plants will thrive in a boggy situation, including meadowsweet *(Filipendula ulmaria),* cardinal flower *(Lobelia cardinalis),* gunnera *(Gunnera manicata),* and sensitive fern *(Onoclea sensibilis).* Some perennial garden favorites, including *Astilbe, Hosta,* and daylily *(Hemerocallis),* also grow exceedingly well in soil that is constantly moist.

The easiest method of developing a bog garden is to excavate a shallow basin near a garden pool or in a separate site. Line the basin with a flexible pool liner or heavy-duty (commercial grade) plastic; then fill it with soil that will hold moisture well. Allow water from the pool to fill the bog. Maintain the water level no more than three inches deep over the top of the soil. If the bog garden is separate, periodically add water with a garden hose, a bucket, or a drip irrigation system if natural rainfall is insufficient.

◀ A boardwalk leads through this extensively planted bog garden that features primroses.

▲ Carnivorous plants such as these pitcher plants can be utilized in southern bog gardens. They trap insects in their tubular pitchers.

Bog gardens should be as broad as they are long. In equal proportions, it's easier to maintain a humid atmosphere which many bog plants prefer. A bog garden that is constructed alongside an existing garden pool might be long and narrow, but even in this situation it should have a wider area to be most effective as well as aesthetically pleasing. Many bog plants are quite large, overpowering a narrow bog.

When constructed next to garden pools, a bog serves as a handsome background to the pool itself when viewed from across the pond. As in planning all water features, have various vantage points in mind. Pathways, patios, terraces, small seating areas, a well-placed bench—all of these help guide people to the best places for quiet contemplation.

▶ Yellow flags (*Iris pseudacorus*), with their flush of bright spring blooms, are striking plants for bog gardens.

BOG GARDENS (CONTINUED)

▲ Bog gardens play host to many plant species that thrive in moist to wet situations. The magenta primroses (*Primula* spp.) in the foreground contrast nicely with the vertical accents of the variegated yellow flag irises (*Iris pseudacorus*) behind them.

▶ This bog garden shows a mix of moisture-loving plants, such as yellow globeflower (*Trollius* ×*cultorum*), pink primula (*Primula vialii*), and lavender orris root (*Iris pallida*) with variegated foliage.

Access is important when thinking about designing and building bog gardens because you must access the plants for various garden chores such as planting, weeding, and trimming. There are a number of solutions to this depending upon the size and location of the bog. Sneak a small path behind the bog garden, so that you can snake your way to various plantings. Surface the path with gravel. Avoid using shredded bark because it may contain natural toxins.

Another good solution is stepping-stones that allow you to cross the bog directly. The easiest method of all is to lay wooden squares down as temporary stepping-stones that are easily moved. Permanent stepping stones might be paving stones or large flat rocks. Anchor them to the bottom of the bog by placing them on concrete block bases. Place the concrete base on several layers of carpet to prevent puncturing the liner.

Living near a bog garden is rewarding, as wildlife will naturally be drawn to it. Frogs and toads that sing each spring find a bog garden a pleasant place to live. Songbirds gather in such an oasis to seek water for drinking and bathing. They prefer a spot where water gathers just an inch or so deep. Grow a broad array of plants to attract a variety of species.

In addition to the plants already suggested for bog gardens, royal fern *(Osmunda regalis)* enhances any garden and grows especially well in damp places. Add the tall and elegant Joe-Pye weed *(Eupatorium)* to the drier edges of your bog garden for a handsome display.

▼ **If space is limited, create a bog garden in a container, such as this planting of pitcher plants and mosses.**

DRY CREEKS

▼ Dry creeks may seldom have water flowing in them but they provide the illusion of active water through the careful arrangement of stones and rocks.

Dry creeks and streambeds create the illusion of the real thing, implying that they are natural streams during the dry season. Make them sinuous and winding; then plant with small bushy shrubs and perennials that alternately expose and hide the dry creek, just like natural plantings along a real creek or stream. A dry streambed need not be deep to present the illusion of a water-filled stream.

To build a dry creek you need rocks placed over landscape fabric to prevent weed growth. A good-size boulder or three serve as an interesting focal point. Sink the stone partially into the ground to provide a more natural appearance. (Placing plants or rocks in odd numbers is aesthetically more pleasing.)

To have a natural-looking dry creek, study a few local natural waterways and steal a bit of design from nature. When larger rocks edge the

▶ **Massed plantings of perennials border this dry creek, adding to the suggestion that this is a natural streambed.**

feature and smaller rocks and pebbles make up the bed of the dry creek, it can be hard to believe that this is not a real stream. Wind the dry stream around larger rocks or intertwine small streambeds to create a braided effect.

If you have the good fortune to have some slope to your property, take advantage of that by digging the dry creek bed to follow the path you want rainwater to drain. Direct the streambed to gardens that need ample water. If runoff already has created a channel, use that as the basis of your dry creek. Line the channel with landscape fabric to eliminate weeds. Complete the desired effect with decorative stones and a variety of plants.

▼ **The bridge over this dry creek surely implies running water. The location next to a lotus pond further suggests the presence of water.**

CONTAINER WATER GARDENS

For beautiful container water gardens, you need three things. You need the right setting for displaying a container. You need appropriate and handsome containers that are watertight. And, of course, you need the right combinations of plants.

▼ A container water garden is easy to construct with water-loving plants attractively arranged in a handsome concrete container. It can serve as a focal point in an entry garden.

◀ In addition to serving as an architectural focal point, a container water garden can serve a simpler role as a decorative piece on a porch or patio table.

A sunny front entranceway or porch of a classic home is a good site for a matched pair of large formal urns holding plantings of water iris *(Iris)* and water hyacinth *(Eichhornia crassipes)*. A wide place in a paved pathway makes room for a rustic whiskey barrel. Build a patio or terrace with enough room for container gardens and the patio furniture.

A simple flagstone or paving stone can serve as the base for a container full of water plants. A section of log or telephone pole can serve as a pillar for a container water garden. A series of three logs of differing heights is a pleasing setting for three elegant container water gardens. Stone pillars and pedestals are available at many garden centers. When using pedestals or pillars as bases for your container water garden, make certain that they are large enough and sturdy enough to hold the containers without tipping over.

Container water gardening is comparatively carefree. Select a handsome waterproof container, add water, and then plant and enjoy. Keep the water level near the rim, and that's about all there is to it. Miniature water lilies and lotuses are a joy to own. Bog plants, hardy water plants, tropical water plants—all are adaptable to container gardens.

The container can be almost anything that holds water. (Avoid unlined copper; it can be toxic.) If the container is not waterproof, seal it with waterproofing or add a waterproof liner. Ready-made liners are available for half whiskey barrels.

Spitting ornamental fountains can be a part of these gardens. Use a submersible pump and filter with your container water garden if necessary. With the right mix of plants and fish in the right-size container you can establish an environmentally balanced ecosystem.

CONTAINER WATER GARDENS (CONTINUED)

▼ A combination of a fountain, pebbles, and a handsome container serves as an attractive accent in just about any room of the home. It also adds pleasing sounds to the ambience of the setting.

The simplest way to bring water inside is to have a containerized water garden. This could be a garden that you enjoy outdoors during warm months, or might be a containerized water garden put together specifically for a place indoors.

Growing tropical water plants in an indoor feature creates an exotic effect. If your home has an atrium or glassed-in porch, this would be an ideal site for a constructed pool of mortared brick or paving stones. Once a flexible liner is installed, a small pool is ready for planting. Consider building in a pump that is both artistic and functional as it oxygenates the water.

Surround the pool with containerized plants that blend well with the ones growing in the pool. An indoor pool is a good place for miniature lilies and lotuses as well as a few other floating and marginal plants. Small fish add to the charm of this type of installation.

In addition to its role as a beautiful part of indoor decor, an indoor pool can serve as a

◀ **This formal fountain in the front hall of the home adds a special touch that underlines the formality of the setting.**

conservatory for tender tropical water plants that have spent the warm season outdoors. In the fall when the weather starts to cool, take clippings of such tender plants as water hyacinth *(Eichhornia crassipes),* fairy moss *(Azolla filiculoides),* and parrot's feather *(Myriophyllum aquaticum).* If you provide aquatic plants with bright light they should thrive in the indoor setting, and you can take them outside once again when spring arrives.

As with other water features, the only limits to the beauty and unique qualities of an indoor water feature are your imagination and your budget. Study other indoor water features and learn from them what most appeals to you before embarking on your own project.

▶ **This indoor water feature combines luxurious ferns and baby tears with the appeal of a trickling channel of water to keep them moist.**

CHAPTER HIGHLIGHTS

This chapter describes the role of water features in the landscape and explains how to site a water feature, develop a plan, calculate water volume, and choose materials for the garden.

DESIGNING AND PLANNING WATER GARDENS

A well-planned and carefully constructed water feature enhances the value of your property as well as the enjoyment of your home. Learn how to develop a plan and do the math to calculate surface area and water volume. You will need to know these things in order to purchase the right amounts and kinds of materials and equipment.

These days, with new materials and equipment, it's easier to create water features, from pools to fountains to rain gardens, than it would have been 20 years ago. Yet because most water features are permanent additions to the landscape, it does pay to go slowly and plan carefully. Large excavations are not easily undone.

Learn about materials that are available and what their comparative costs are. Find out what products retail mail-order catalogs have available. Get to know local stores and nurseries that specialize in water plants, supplies, and materials. Find out who in your area is good at building water features. Take the time to follow up on references so that you can see work that has been done for others.

ROLE OF WATER GARDENS

▼ A water feature such as this handsome fountain that is enhanced by surrounding plants adds distinction to an otherwise plain setting.

Water is a garden feature in itself. Whether silent in a mysterious dark pool or brightly reflecting the sunlight in jewel-like droplets of water from a fountain, water brings new dimensions to a garden. Water can serve as a mirror, reflecting sculpture, elegant plants, or clouds and sky. Water in a pool, stream, or fountain can serve as a focal point in the garden, drawing attention to the water feature and its surrounding plants.

Water features can serve as a screen, shielding a backyard living area from nearby streets and neighbors.

Fountains and streams are excellent at buffering noise pollution. The sound of moving water effectively erases the noise of the neighborhood, covers up the sounds of traffic, and brings tranquil peace to your backyard.

A garden pool brings a new appreciation for gardening different from garden beds or borders. The palette of garden plants suited to life alongside, in, or on water is evergrowing. The variety of both hardy and tropical plants available to water gardeners is extensive. Choose a few plants appropriate for the setting, and gardening chores will be easier than if you were gardening on dry land.

Water features in gardens are magnets for wildlife, especially birds and amphibians. No sooner have you filled your garden pool with water than news will spread among local songbirds. Provide them with shallow water at one end of your water feature and you will have colorful visitors stopping by for drinks and baths. If you live in the suburbs or country, your water feature soon will attract frogs, toads, and salamanders, native insect eaters that will move in and share your yard. There's nothing like the trills and croaks of frogs and toads to welcome spring.

An added attraction of a well-designed and executed water feature is that it quite likely will increase the value of your property and enhance its appeal to prospective buyers.

▲ Combining good elements of design, such as this fountain, pool, and decorative tile, results in a water feature that is more enjoyable.

▼ Miniature water lilies in a small containerized water garden draw the eye with their classic forms.

Experts and Sources

Enthusiasm is wonderful, but don't move too quickly. You undoubtedly will be living with your water features for a long time, so it pays to cover all the bases. At this stage check with friends who have water gardens and in the Yellow Pages in search of reliable retail outlets for water feature contractors and supplies. Use the Internet to locate specialty suppliers of water gardening resources and equipment.

If you have a public garden nearby with water features, ask staff members for names of suppliers, contractors, and others who specialize in installing water features. You may wisely decide that you are going to need professional help in building your water feature–be prepared by doing the homework now. Once you have a few names, ask for references as well as ballpark ranges of costs. Check the references carefully.

▲ Rely on the expertise of a water garden supplier with a reputation for helpfulness and reliability. Ask as many questions as possible.

◄ Visit a water garden supplier and consider the options in equipment and accessories. Ask for product brochures with specifications so you can compare your options.

Increasing numbers of retail stores specialize in water garden merchandise or have a water garden department. Because water gardens continue to increase in popularity, plant nurseries often include a full line of water feature supplies, fish, and water plants in their stock. The staff people at nurseries usually can answer questions you may have or else they know where to find the answers. If the nursery has display gardens with water features, you can learn a lot by studying them.

Gather a list of retail mail-order businesses that specialize in water feature equipment, materials, plants, or fish. If you can't find what you need at your favorite local nursery, mail-order suppliers are a good alternative.

Search for a local water gardening club or society. If there isn't one in your town, start one and invite interested friends and neighbors to join. You can learn a lot about water gardening from others with similar interests.

▼ Consulting with experts before you begin construction of a water feature often will save both time and money in the long run.

Siting

Carefully consider where to site your water feature. Pools and ponds are comparatively large and thus difficult to undo. Those larger than 4×6 feet and 18 inches or more deep will be easier to maintain and keep ecologically balanced. Avoid the mistake of planning a water feature that is on a scale too large for the property. Keep features in scale with your home and existing landscaping.

Fit formal water features into the existing symmetry of buildings and outdoor living areas. The view from a patio, terrace, or other vantage point can make or break the aesthetics of the finished pond, pool, or other water feature. Plan ahead to assure that the site offers the best views of the water feature from these high-use areas.

Sunlight is important for a water garden that includes plants. Most aquatic plants require at least a half-day of sun. On the other hand, too

▶ Siting your water garden away from trees helps minimize the maintenance involved in continually scooping leaves, twigs, and other debris out of the water.

much sun can cause algae buildup. An ideal location might have shade at one end of the pool or receive full morning sun and some afternoon shade.

If the property slopes, fit the water feature into a location partway down the hill. Avoid the top of the grade or the low spots into which rainwater drains. To minimize problems from excess water, avoid placing pools or ponds next to a house, under eaves, or close to downspouts. For convenience, think of both water and electrical sources. Are they near enough for easy access?

Consider the location of existing trees. Deciduous trees can drop leaves into the water, requiring frequent cleanup. Tree roots growing under a pool or pond can cause problems by puncturing the liner and causing leaks.

▲ **It is possible and reasonable for households that include children and pets to have a water feature as well.**

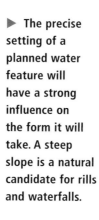 ▶ **The precise setting of a planned water feature will have a strong influence on the form it will take. A steep slope is a natural candidate for rills and waterfalls.**

DEVELOPING A PLAN

▲ **When preparing a site plan, measure the distance among key features in the landscape, such as the house, walkways, and planting areas.**

This is the time to get out the pencil and notebook and put dimensions, orientation, and other specifics down on paper. Draw sketches showing the relationship of the water feature to existing buildings, trees, and paved areas. Make the drawings to scale on graph paper. This is particularly important if you plan to construct pathways or allow space for tables, benches, or other garden accessories.

Mark the outline of the water feature with rope or a garden hose. Move it around until you are pleased with the dimensions, shape, and site. If you like, mark the outline with chalk or water-soluble spray paint, available from hardware stores. Note that a pool or pond that is at least 18 inches deep with a surface area of 30 square feet or more will be large enough to achieve a balance between plants and fish. Measure the dimensions and put them onto

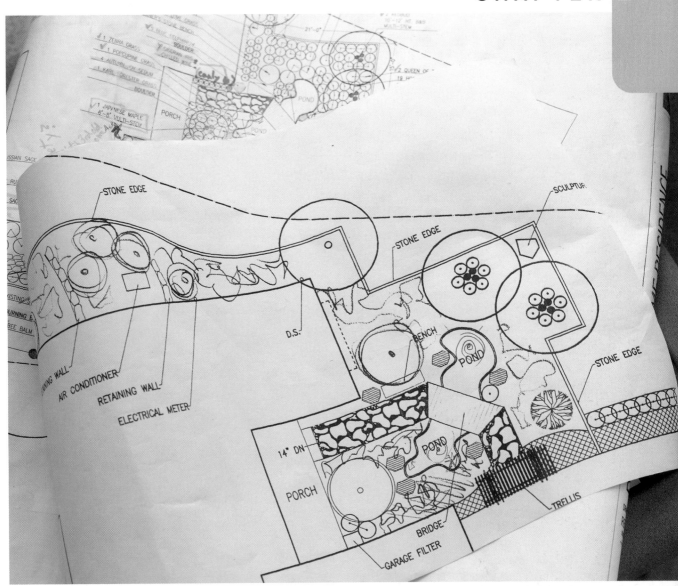

your scale drawing. Include suggestions for plants, both in the water feature and for the landscape surrounding it.

Next develop a side view or cutaway view of the pool or pond that indicates depth and plant shelves for containerized aquatic plants, if plants are part of your plan. A koi (colorful Japanese carp) pond often does not have plants because koi may feast on aquatic plants as a major part of their diet. Locate the plant shelves at the appropriate depth for the types of plants you will grow. Hardy water lilies and lotuses require water that is 18–30 inches deep, and marginal plants require a water depth of 0–3 inches. You may want to make the center of the excavation

deep enough to prevent the water there from freezing solid during winter. (This depth varies depending on your climate). This provides refuge for frogs and fish, such as goldfish.

Budget may be a consideration in developing a water garden. Various stages of development will call for a variety of skills and costs. Make note on the plan you are drawing of possible stages of development that could be spread out over several years. For instance, the first year might be allotted to excavation and basic water feature construction. The second year could be devoted to landscaping with plants, and the final year to construction of pathways, seating, and other hardscaping details.

▲ Save time and potential problems by enlisting the services of a landscape design professional who can complete a site plan for a water garden.

CONTAINERS

Planning is important even for simple container water features. Water is heavy. So are many containers. Limit placement to sites that are structurally able to take the weight. If you plan to put a container water garden on a porch, balcony, or deck, you may need to check with an engineer to determine whether the site is strong enough to carry the extra weight of the water feature. Set a container water garden on a firm, sturdy foundation. If it is permanently placed in one spot in a garden or patio, build a concrete base and cement the feature to it.

▲ A containerized triple bamboo fountain lends height and an Oriental flavor to the garden setting.

► This trickling fountain features a sturdy ceramic jar overflowing into a shallow reservoir lined with stones.

Half whiskey barrels and wash tubs are easy containers to work with. A whiskey barrel may leak. Although soaking may swell the wood enough to prevent leakage, it is far better to line the barrel with a flexible liner or a ready-made rigid liner. Wash tubs also make good rustic containers for small water features. Consider other potential containers—stainless steel sinks, bathtubs, large buckets, or decorative pots. Let your imagination run wild.

Look for ready-made kits that include all you need to put together a containerized water feature. They are available in all sorts of styles and sizes. Many have built-in pumps and fountains. Some are constructed around small statues, figures, or animals, so that you have a handsome feature as well as the added attraction of the fountain's sound.

Add sketches of the containerized water feature to the scale drawing of your garden, noting dimensions, including height. Visualize the feature in that spot. Before you add water, move the container around, fine-tuning the exact location until you are pleased. Only then, proceed with permanent installation, and fill it with water. Or place the container water garden on a plant dolly so that it can easily be moved around to take advantage of seasonal changes in light or to show it off for special occasions.

▲ A half whiskey barrel will hold a sizeable collection of floating and emergent water plants. Here the maroon foliage of cardinal flower combines with blooming iris and water lilies. Floating water lettuce and feathery milfoil provide textural contrast.

IN-GROUND WATER GARDENS

▲ The beginning of in-ground water garden construction calls for outlining the pool perimeter carefully with a rope, landscape paint, or a hose.

Designing and planning for an in-ground garden feature is more complicated than that for container water gardens. Changing the grade, and using excavated soil in a creative way take careful consideration if the water feature is to enhance the property.

At this stage you have decided what kind of in-ground water feature you want for your property. In a notebook, list the roles you want your pool, pond, or stream to play. If you want a koi pond, requirements will be quite different from those of a garden pool or pond that will have a few goldfish and is constructed mainly to display plants. Similarly, the requirements differ for a reflecting pool or for a pool that is constructed primarily to enhance a fountain of considerable size and artistic merit.

Build koi ponds 2–4 feet deep for best results. Koi ponds often have no plants for two reasons. First, these are showy fish that you'll want to keep in sight as much as possible and, second, koi may eat the plants unless the koi are only 4–5 inches long when you stock them in the pond and you do not feed them. Since koi ponds usually include aeration and filtration systems, there is little need for plants to help balance the system. Include vertical sides to the koi pond and provide hiding places to discourage fish predators.

▲ Take advantage of opportunities to visit water gardens and ask the gardeners for advice. Learn from their successes and avoid their mistakes in your garden.

Pools or ponds that are constructed to display plants, on the other hand, may also have little need for filters and aerators if the plants and fish establish an ecological balance. To display various plants, plan on a pond that is 18–30 inches deep in the center. Use shelves constructed around the pool at a couple of depths to display other kinds of marginal and submerged plants. Build in a 2-percent slope to the bottom of the pond to make draining it easier. Include fish, other than koi, and floating plants for a balanced system.

▶ Before you plant or stock your water garden, research the diverse options available. Visit local pond stores to see the plants and fish yourself before deciding what to include.

▼ **A small reflecting pool makes an entryway more inviting. Plants placed nearby gain emphasis through their reflections in the still water.**

Reflecting pools or those that primarily serve as the basis for an ornamental fountain can be quite shallow. Because they do not have to support animal or plant life, you can treat the water with chemicals to keep it clear and to control algae. Although pools such as these are not intended to support plant and animal life, planning for them is no less important. Water circulation is critical for shallow pools. Areas with stagnant water can grow algae even if you use chlorine to minimize algal growth because the chemicals fail to reach the dead area.

Make certain liners fit properly. The pools should blend with the existing landscape. Think through planting needs so as to enhance both the pool and the surrounding landscape.

Whatever the role you intend for your pool, get it on graph paper scaled properly. The more accurate and detailed your drawings are, the easier it will be to continue the project. You will be able to accurately figure areas and volumes. These numbers are vital to purchasing the right amount of materials, the right size of liner, an appropriate pump, and to maintain the pool.

◀ This two-level pool with its upper reflecting pool and lower-level bubbling fountain lends an air of elegance to the patio.

Once your scale drawings are complete, check with your city or county building inspector. Building codes vary. You may need a building permit for your water feature. Abide by laws governing water in the landscape. Some cities and towns require a fence around any water feature that is more than 18 inches deep. Consider property setback requirements, especially on smaller lots. Knowing both the requirements and restrictions of a community can be of major importance when planning a sizeable water feature.

Check the requirements for electrical systems. A licensed electrician may be needed to set up connections for your pool pumps, filters, aerators, and lighting. Although low-voltage electrical accessories for water gardens are available, even they can be dangerous.

▶ The ornamental fence with its unique arched gate surrounds the water feature in a beautiful manner while at the same time providing secure access to the water feature.

MAKING CALCULATIONS

LINER AREA

Liner length = pool length + (2× pool depth) + 2 feet

Liner width = pool width + (2× pool depth) + 2 feet

Liner area = liner length × liner width

Remember: It is better to have too much overlap than not enough.

In order to purchase pool liners and other materials, you'll need to know the surface area of your new pond. In order to purchase the appropriate filters, pump, aerator, and other accessories, you need to calculate the volume of the pond. In the case of pumps, you also need to determine how far the pump has to lift the water.

If you have drawn your water feature to scale you can make the calculations on your own. If you're uncertain of your math skills, have a knowledgeable friend double check your figures, or visit a retail nursery or water garden supply store with your plan in hand and get some professional advice.

Although you have all the dimensions of the pool on your scale drawing, measure again once digging is completed in case the excavation is not quite accurate to your plan. Nothing would be worse than finding out as installation is nearing completion that the liner is too small. As the old saying goes, "measure twice, cut once."

FIGURING THE WATER VOLUME OF A POOL

For figuring pump sizes, and to help when treating water with chemicals, you need to know how many gallons of water your pond holds. Here's how to do that:

Calculate all dimensions in feet. First calculate the surface area of the pond, as shown. Multiply the surface area by the average depth of the pond to find volume. Multiply volume by 7.48 to find capacity in gallons. For irregularly shaped ponds, multiply the length (L) × width (W) × depth (D) × 6.7 to get an estimate of the number of gallons of water in the pond.

SURFACE AREA OF RECTANGULAR OR SQUARE POND: Multiply width (W) by length (L) to find surface area.

SURFACE AREA OF A CIRCULAR POND: Measure the length from center to edge (radius [R]). Multiply that figure by itself, and then by 3.14 to find surface area.

SURFACE AREA OF AN OBLONG POND: Divide the pond into a square (or rectangle) and two half circles. Calculate the area of the square; then consider the two half circles as one full circle and calculate its surface area.

SURFACE AREA OF OVAL POND: Measure from the center to the farthest edge, then from the center to the nearest edge. Multiply the first figure by the second, and the result by 3.14 to find surface area.

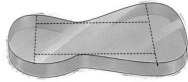

SURFACE AREA OF AN IRREGULAR POND: Divide the pond into simple units (*above*, a rectangle, triangles, and semicircles) and figure the area of each.

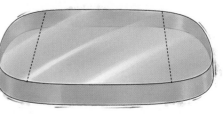

Choosing Materials

▲ This detail of a pool constructed with a flexible liner shows how natural the pond can appear when plants such as irises, ferns, and rhododendrons soften the edges.

Constructing water features has become easier and less expensive than years ago. The choices of materials for building an in-ground water feature were limited. The usual choice was concrete, a difficult material to work with. Concrete, in time, cracks causing leakage.

The development of rigid plastics, flexible plastics, and synthetic rubber has made pool construction easier, more cost effective, and longer lasting. Make certain the liner is of food or pond quality. Some other liners have antifungal and antibacterial agents that are harmful to aquatic plants and animals. If you

▼ A rigid-form pool provides a more formal impression with its geometric angles. You can, however, soften this effect by using plants in an imaginative way to camouflage the corners.

are reasonably handy with do-it-yourself projects, you have just about all of the skills needed to construct an in-ground water feature with a preformed or flexible liner. To complete your project, manufacturers make fiberglass or composite pools, waterfalls, streams and cascades, fountains, and artificial rocks.

Today's technology also offers long-lasting plastic and composite lumber made from recycled materials. Although the first recycled building materials were lacking in several respects, today's version is versatile and easy to use. It comes in different colors and textures. Texture is particularly useful if plastic or composite lumber is used to construct decking—it is not slippery, so it is safer. Of course, recycled materials are rot-resistant, so they will need infrequent maintenance and replacement when used in association with water.

Plastic pumps, filters, clarifiers, fountain heads, flexible tubing, and statuary have played a large role in making the construction of pools, ponds, waterfalls, and streams easier and less expensive.

▼ A square concrete garden pool with symmetrical plantings, formal bench, and classically themed statue are ideal for a formal walled garden.

FLEXIBLE LINERS

The development of EPDM (ethylene propylene diene monomer), a synthetic rubber, was a boon to water feature installation. In the past, recommended materials for flexible liners included PVC (polyvinyl chloride). While you still can purchase PVC in some places, it is not nearly as popular as EPDM.

It's easy to see why pond-quality EPDM is so popular. It is highly stable and formulated to be safe for both plants and fish. This is an important factor, as some plastic materials leach substances harmful to animal and plant life.

EPDM is flexible at temperatures from −40°F to 175°F. This means that you can install an EPDM liner at any time of year. Further, it contains no plasticizers that make other liner materials brittle with age. Plasticizers can result in cracks or splits as the material ages, threatening the integrity of the water feature. In addition, EPDM has high resistance to the harmful effects of ultraviolet (UV) radiation, ozone, and other environmental conditions.

The flexibility of EPDM allows great creativity in design of water features. While preformed rigid liners

◀ **EPDM flexible liner conforms to the shape of pool shelves, shallow ledges, and deeper excavations.**

and containers allow but one shape, this flexible material easily fits the contours of just about any pool or pond design.

EPDM has high elongation, which is a great capability for expansion and contraction. What this means is that if earth movement occurs or if tree roots expand beneath the liner, EPDM's high elongation allows it to stretch over the objects.

Professionals recommend a 2-foot liner overlap for edging a pool, especially if you're building a water feature for the first time. Purchase an underlayment of the same dimensions to give the liner protection from rocks, roots, and other potentially harmful objects.

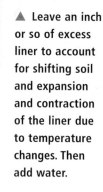

▲ Leave an inch or so of excess liner to account for shifting soil and expansion and contraction of the liner due to temperature changes. Then add water.

◄ Placing the coping to hide the edges of the flexible liner and installing plants add finishing touches for a garden pool.

RIGID POOLS

E ven though they allow little flexibility in design and application, there are good reasons for using rigid or semirigid pools. They serve as a beginner pool if you're unsure what water gardening is all about. They offer a chance to experiment with a few plants and fish and discover whether this kind of gardening is for you. Modern materials, improved technology, and improved design add up to make some of these ready-made pools suited to even the most demanding gardener.

▲ **A rectangular aboveground pool set against garden beds nicely echoes the lines of the arbor and fence. By using wood for all three projects, this homeowner has unified the landscape through the choice of materials.**

Fiberglass and bonded resins are among the most durable materials for rigid water features. Even though these are comparatively small pools, invest in a quality unit. Fiberglass lasts longer than less expensive material, and is easier to repair if damaged.

▶ **An aboveground water garden with a rigid liner makes an ideal site for water-loving plants such as rodgersia and arrowhead.**

Some preformed pools are simply rigid black plastic molded into a particular shape. Preformed streams and cascades are available. Plastic basins and pools may be interconnected on a slope so that you have the illusion of a wonderful wild stream. More complex units are molded to look like natural rock-lined streams and cascades. These are easier to install than putting down flexible liners and then placing stones and gravel in natural ways.

▼ **A two-level rigid pool in the familiar kidney shape can be the basis for an attractive informal water feature.**

CONTAINERS

Many items that hold water can be transformed into containers for water gardens. The important things to consider are that the container be watertight and that its inner surface be inert. If you have doubts about the inner surface, paint the inside of the container with silicone, hard polyethylene, or other coating recommended for such use.

Even a birdbath on a pedestal can serve as a water garden. The birds will continue to visit even if it has small water plants growing in the basin. Visit a farm supply store to open your eyes to the various shapes and sizes of stock watering tanks that could serve as water features. Place the stock tank on the surface or sink it into the ground. Accessorize the tank with pots of annual flowers, tropical foliage plants, or with beds of perennials installed around the edges.

If you wish to have a small water feature inside a basket or other container that holds no water, improvise by putting a heavy-duty plastic bag or piece of pond liner inside and then plant some aquatic marginal plants. This will not be a permanent water feature, but it will be good for one growing season.

◀ **An old bathtub serves as a whimsical garden pool with its showerhead fountain spraying a "rubber duck" topiary.**

◀ A handsome glazed ceramic bowl serves as a miniature water garden with its planting of water lettuce. It makes a good-looking decorative piece for the summer picnic table.

▼ An antique water tub makes a fine container for a mix of water-loving species. If it is copper, paint the inside to prevent harmful metals from leaching into the water.

Old bathtubs and sinks are likely prospects for creating a water feature. Both are watertight. If the light ceramic finish bothers you, coat the piece with black waterproofing pool paint. An old claw-foot bathtub makes a light-hearted water feature standing on its own. A bathtub can hold a couple of miniature waterlilies and several other aquatic plants. It's perfect for a few small fish. (The usual ratio is about 2 inches of fish—excluding the tail—for each square foot of water surface.)

Don't forget washtubs and whiskey barrel halves, old standbys for quick and easy containerized water gardens. They are about equal size and can be finished in similar ways. Make a handsome garden focal point by planting one of them with a few carefully chosen aquatic plants.

ACCESSORIES

Once the water feature is completed, think about accessories that will enhance it, making it more comfortable and useful. These include seating—chairs, benches, and tables—and hardscape features such as bridges, decks, and piers. Make certain wooden features contain no toxins that may leach into the water. Add a touch of class to your water garden by choosing some artwork—a sculpture, decorative boulder, or beautiful piece of driftwood.

Use the scaled drawing that you prepared for the construction of the water feature to develop plans for any decking, a pier, or new patio.

Once you decide what kind of table and seating arrangement you like, work those into the drawings as well. You may find it handy to cut out a scaled outline of your table and seating. Move the cutouts around on the plan until you reach a pleasing arrangement, then glue or tape them down.

Keep your water garden furniture and hardscape features appropriate in size and style to the rest of the water garden and to the entire landscape. Massive tables, for instance, do not fit in well with small-scale pools and fountains. Color also can be important to the mood of the

▼ An arched bridge, available ready-made in some water garden shops, is a handsome accent for a garden pool.

garden. Use pastel pinks, creams, blues, or greens for a peaceful oasis. Hot pink, bright reds, yellows, and oranges are appropriate to set a festive tone.

Paths are another important category of water feature accessories. Plan them with a purpose. They can lead one from one place to another or to a particularly lovely vantage point. Paths provide access through a garden so that you can care for plantings. Paths may be formal or informal, depending upon the impression you wish to make. Stone, concrete, or paving blocks create a formal look. Pebbles, wood chips, or bark lend a natural ambience.

Uplighting adds drama to this formal garden fountain and pool.

An artistic bench provides the crowning touch to this beautiful garden pool, providing the perfect place for a quiet conversation among friends.

Water Source

When planning a water feature, consider how water will be transported to the feature. If water comes from an approved private well, there is little worry about its chemical quality, but it may require oxygenation to counteract low levels of dissolved oxygen. If your water originates from a community water system, chances are it is treated with a chemical such as chloramine.

Chemicals may be removed in a couple of ways. If the water sits for several days before use, chlorine dissipates into the air. Chloramine, however, remains in water for months. Use a chloramine remover if your water supplier adds chloramine. The chloramine treatment also removes the chlorine. Because chloramine remover releases ammonia into the water, also treat the water with pond bacteria to remove excess ammonia.

Acidity or alkalinity of the water is extremely important to the success of any water feature that includes plants or fish. If using a swimming pool water testing kit, maintain water pH between 7.5 and 10.5. For most accurate test results, sample the water early in the evening when carbon dioxide levels are lower. Water-quality test kits are easier to use than they used to be. In addition to testing for pH, check for absence of chlorine and chloramine, and keep levels of nitrate and ammonia low.

◄ **Filling a water feature with the garden hose is an easy and pleasant task. Avoid adding tap water directly to the pond. Slowly add water through the waterfalls or filter to prevent fish from playing in the bubbling water. They may burn their gill plates if the chloramine content of the water is 4–5 parts per million or more.**

The easiest way to transport water to a small feature is a handy garden bucket, especially if it is in a far corner of the garden. A trusty garden hose is the most common means of transporting water to a pool. During hot summer days, as much as an inch of water evaporates from a pool or pond. Proportionately more evaporates from a fountain or waterfall, so a convenient source of water is important. Although it usually is not necessary, you can install piping and faucets to make the water source more convenient for refilling your pond.

Automatic water devices operate on the toilet tank principle to keep water at a desired level. Contact an expert and get bids on costs and installation if you wish to add this level of convenience to your water feature.

▶ **An in-ground water source next to the pool provides an efficient means of topping off a water garden feature.**

▲ **A lightweight bucket makes it easy to add a small amount of water to a pond or pool.**

ELECTRICAL SOURCE

Electricity and water together can spell danger. Be careful with electrical equipment to be used along with a water feature, especially if tapping into your household electrical system. Never use an extension cord to power up pumps, filters, and lights for a water garden or water feature. Even those designed for outdoor use provide a potential hazard when used near water. Many communities have ordinances requiring a licensed electrician do any electrical installation work. It's usually safest to call upon a licensed electrician whether or not your community requires it.

Low-voltage pumps and lights are made with transformers that convert household current to a less dangerous voltage. They come with detailed instructions explaining what to do. Solar-powered lights do a good job of lighting paths and pools.

◀ Install an electrical junction box that is convenient to the water garden yet protected from the elements. Check your local zoning code requirements for the proper distance to locate the electrical source from water.

▲ An outlet cover helps shelter plugged-in power cords from rain, dew, or sprinklers.

General guidelines for supplying electricity to garden features include the following:

■ Keep electrical outlets 5 feet or more away from the water feature.

■ Provide watertight housings for electrical outlets.

■ Run electrical cable through protective PVC sheathing.

■ Bury the cable as deeply as local building codes or ordinances require.

■ Use a ground fault circuit interrupter (GFCI) that cuts off the power if the electrical power is compromised for even 30 milliseconds to protect the entire circuit.

■ Use contact circuit breakers in outdoor sockets for further safety.

If your water feature needs electrical power more than 100 feet from the house, a licensed electrician may need to install a special

▲ Adding lighting to this small pool and fountain creates a magical effect.

distribution system in a watertight housing. If you make this or any other electrical adaptations, be sure to add their locations and descriptions to the scaled drawings of your plan. By doing so, you can protect the underground cable from digging accidents and make it easier to make any changes in the future.

PUMPS

If you have a stream, cascade, waterfall, or fountain, choose a pump that can handle the load that the water feature requires. You can keep water clear in a pool or pond without a pump or aerator if you keep fish to the required ratio and have enough submerged plants to provide oxygenation. If you want greater latitude in number and sizes of fish and plants, you may need to use pumps and filters.

Some water feature kits come with pumps and necessary tubing included. Such kits are easy to install without professional help.

Choosing the right pump can be challenging since there are several types and many sizes. By now you should have figured the number of gallons of water in your pool or pond. If you are planning to have a waterfall, cascade, or descending stream, you should have calculated the rise that a pump will have to lift the water.

▶ **This submersible pump has been pulled from its housing for maintenance on the pump and the stream that it powers.**

Pump manufacturers have charts that will help you choose the right pump if you have those figures. If you need only to filter the water, choose a pump that is strong enough to circulate the entire volume of water every one to two hours. Those numbers will be on the outside of the package.

Pumps come in two main types, submersible and external. Submersible pumps are placed in the pool, have built-in filters to keep debris from the motor (clean them regularly), are cooled by

▲ An aboveground pump, housed in this protective black box, calls for its own dedicated line from the circuit breaker, necessitating professional installation.

the water, and are comparatively easy to install. Select a submersible pump in the size and capacity matched to your water features.

External pumps are similar to those made for swimming pools, and all but the smallest ones require a 220-volt electrical circuit for operation. If you decide to use an external pump, have a professional install it.

Aeration and Filtration

Filtration may be needed to keep pool water clear. Water gardens dedicated to keeping koi usually require a filtration system because the koi not only eat plants but they also keep the water in turmoil by rooting in the pond bottom. Filters remove debris and convert waste substances to less harmful materials.

Mechanical filters use materials such as silica sand, chemical filters use materials such as activated charcoal, and biological filters use beneficial bacteria to clear the water. Water circulation is needed for any good filtration system to work. Therefore, you need an adequate pump with the right diameter piping to assure proper water flow. Filtered water returning to the pool creates a mild current.

Use a skimmer that removes surface debris, such as leaves, as part of your filtration system.

An all-purpose filtration system consists of a large plastic container, with fittings that attach to a pump and flow back into the pool or pond. Some commercial filters are easy to disguise. Hide a filtration system behind bushes or in a small shed. Use a submersible pump to push water into the filter.

Ultraviolet (UV) filter systems combine filters with UV sterilizers. UV sterilizers disable and destroy algae, bacteria, and protozoa, which results in clear water with no algae buildup.

Add oxygen to the water through aeration. A waterfall, fountain, or cascade aerates the water in a decorative way. Small submersible aerators are used by commercial fish farms.

These mat aerators will do a good job of adding oxygen to the water too.

Filtration systems and pumps require regular maintenance and protection from freezing weather. Clean the pump intake weekly. Clean the filter and skimmer as needed to maintain efficient operation. In the fall when the water temperature falls below 50°F, remove, clean, and store your system's filter and pump in a cool, dark place in a sealed plastic bag. Reconnect the pump and filter the following spring.

◀ Mechanical filters such as this one do an excellent job of physically removing debris from a garden pool. Even so, you'll need to use a net or vacuum to remove bottom waste every 3–6 months.

▼ Biological filters such as this lava rock biofilter do a good job of keeping the water in garden pools and ponds clear and free of debris.

▲ This healthy pond with its clear, clean water provides a good home for these handsome koi.

TOOLS

Use safety goggles or glasses when working with power saws or other power tools while building your water feature. Wear a dust mask when working with concrete, sawing, or otherwise raising dust. Wear earplugs or ear protectors when using power equipment. Headphone ear protectors are easier to put on and take off, plus they muffle sound better. Wear gloves when handling heavy materials such as stones, rocks, and concrete. Use heavy work boots, preferably with steel toes, if you will be working with stone, bricks, or concrete paving blocks.

▼ **Water garden construction proves simpler when you first gather the tools and equipment you'll need.**

Basic water garden construction tools include a heavy-duty metal rake to level and smooth soil, sand, and gravel. A carpenter's level assures that paved areas are level or have a slight grade for drainage. You'll also find it handy to make certain the outer edge of the pool is level. Use a level in conjunction with a board as long as the width of the pool to make certain the pool edge is level around the entire perimeter. A line level that clips onto a cord or line is an alternative to the carpenter's level. Garden hose or rope is good for initial outlining of water features. Stakes are handy to more permanently mark outlines and limitations.

Measuring tapes 25–100 feet in length are necessary for planning as well as construction. A straight edge or 3- to 4-foot-long board will be useful in leveling pond edges. A long-handle, round-nose shovel is good for excavating soil. A square-nose spade is best for forming vertical sides and flat bottoms of pools and ponds. A tarpaulin is useful for temporarily storing excavated soil. A wheelbarrow or garden cart is essential for transporting equipment and heavy materials such as rocks and sand.

▶ **Protect your back from strain or injury by enlisting the help of a heavy-duty wheelbarrow to haul weighty materials, such as soil and rocks.**

CHAPTER HIGHLIGHTS

This chapter discusses whether or not to call in a professional installer, and then tells you how to prepare and construct pool sites. You'll also learn how to construct other water features, including fountains, waterfalls, rills, rain gardens, dry creeks, and bog gardens.

CONSTRUCTING WATER GARDENS

Now you're ready for the real work of constructing your water feature. You've done the research and developed the plan in scale on graph paper. Having this detailed plan will pay off during construction. Use copies of the plan on-site so that the original does not get dirty or muddy while you're building.

Make one final check of the plan, the materials, your equipment, and tools. Purchase any missing items. Keep all of them close at hand, ready to begin construction of the water feature.

Plan and construct garden water features with long-range vision. A pool, pond, waterfall, or other water feature will add beauty and serenity to your landscape for many years. The time you spend in developing and then rechecking your ideas and plans will pay off in countless hours of future enjoyment. Spend a little extra time now to ensure your satisfaction with the finished project.

Calling in a Professional

The larger the water feature, the more skills it requires to build. Assess your abilities to excavate accurately and to install electrical accessories such as lighting, pumps, filters, and fountains. Most beginning water garden do-it-yourselfers can manage the construction of a pool or pond that holds 400–800 gallons. Excavating soil is hard work. Laying brick or stone demands muscle power as well as skill. You must construct correctly if the water feature is to be beautiful and function well.

Have you talked to professionals who are in the business of installing water features? Most water-feature contractors are willing to work with homeowners to figure out what the professionals should do and what the homeowner can easily do. You can find these professionals through retail stores that carry water-feature equipment and materials, by asking those who sell fish and aquatic plants, from friends' recommendations, or through the Yellow Pages. Contact several of them and get bids to see if your budget allows a professional installer or contractor to do some of the more difficult work. Be sure to provide the same specifications to each of them to make the bids comparable. Consider the level of experience of the contractor when making your final decision.

Allotting different parts of the construction procedures to yourself and to a professional installer saves a considerable amount over the cost for a professional to do the entire project. Another budget-saver is to have professional installation but spread it out over a couple of years. Construct the basic water feature the first year, and then build associated paths, decks, and other accessories in following years.

▶ Excavating and lining a garden pool is short work for a crew of professional water garden installers, but may require a couple of long weekends for the do-it-yourselfer.

◀ Professional pond installers place rocks on the flexible liner to give a more natural look to the garden pool. Note that the liner is not tightly fitted to the contour of the pond. This provides some give for shifting soil, and allows expansion and contraction during extremes of temperature.

▶ A skimmer with skimmer net and filter pads is part of the water garden package supplied by this professional installation crew.

PREPARING THE SITE

▲ **Before you dig, carefully measure to ensure the pond's correct size and depth.**

One of the first steps to take in any landscaping project is to contact your local utility companies to have their representatives mark the locations of underground cables and lines. This is critical even if the project calls for digging to a depth of only a few inches. In many states, you can contact a one-call service for utility marking, North American One-Call Referral System (888/258-0808).

Utility company representatives mark only company-owned lines. If you have installed an automatic sprinkler system or underground lines for outdoor lighting, you'll need to note those locations yourself. Add utility lines to your scale drawing. If utilities interfere with your plans, either move the water feature or relocate the utility line.

Next remove weeds and other vegetation, including the roots, from the project site. Treat the area with a glyphosate herbicide such as RoundUp a week to 10 days before starting construction. Use a shovel to remove the top couple of inches of turf and soil. Water heavily and pull any remaining roots. Remove the roots of trees and shrubs in the excavation zone. Clear working areas make projects both easier and safer.

Address any drainage problems that result from the excavation. When constructing water features near a home, be sure that the land has a slight slope away from the building. If runoff drains away from the house, you probably will have no problem. Install perforated drainpipe underground to lead runoff away if there is a problem with drainage.

◀ Lay out the water garden's outline using a garden hose and stakes, landscape marking chalk, spray paint, flour, or garden lime.

▶ Use a garden shovel almost horizontally to skim the top couple of inches of soil from the excavation site.

Digging

▼ In order for
the liner to fit
properly it is
important to
excavate the site
of a garden pool
accurately both
in outline and
in depth.

Mark the outline of the pool with garden hose, spray paint, chalk, stakes, or small pegs. Also mark where shelves and any other changes in depth will be. Start digging at the deepest area and gradually work toward the edges. Digging is the most labor-intensive part of building a water feature. For an average-size garden pool, about 8×12 feet, it will take one person a couple of weekends to excavate, construct, and set up properly.

Dig when the soil is not too dry or too wet. If the soil is too dry, set up a sprinkler to moisten it before digging. For larger projects, hire a backhoe or bulldozer operator. You will be surprised at the amount of soil that comes out of the pool site. If your plan calls for a simple pool, level with the surrounding ground line,

arrange to have the excavated soil hauled away. If you plan to include a stream or fountain, use the soil to build a berm and add the necessary changes in grade.

Once the deepest part of the pool has been dug to the specified level, begin shaping any shelves that are part of the plan. Plant shelves should be 12–18 inches in width. A transitional shallow area around the entire perimeter is a good solution for using marginal plants. These shallower areas are good safety features to prevent small children from accidentally falling into deeper water. Save the final shaping for the very end. Use a straight-nose spade to make a smooth bottom, shelves, and sides.

If the plan includes outdoor lighting, a pump, or other electrical equipment, call in a licensed electrician. If the plumbing aspects of the plan are beyond your capabilities, call in a plumber. Make sure that all underground installations are complete before proceeding to the next stage of construction. Note the location and depth of underground installations on your master plan.

DIGGING A POND

Remove sod or the top layer of plant growth across the entire pond area. During excavation, fully remove tree and shrub roots. Dig a rim 3 inches deep and 12 inches wide outside the actual pond outline. The edge of the pond liner will lie in this rim, held in place by stone.

CREATING VARIED DEPTHS

Make one ledge 12 inches wide and between 3 and 6 inches below grade. This ledge will support the stone and plants that naturalize the edge. This edge doesn't need to go all the way around the pond. You can make one area taper gradually deeper, like a gravel beach into a lake.

Make another ledge at least 10 inches below the first, 12–18 inches wide. Excavate the center section so that the pond is at least 24 inches deep. In regions where winter temperatures drop below –20°F, dig the pond 40 inches deep if you want to keep the pond from freezing solid so fish can overwinter. (You can use a stock-tank heater in a shallower pond to keep fish through the winter too.)

LEVELING

Level edges of a pool or pond have an important bearing on the final look of the water feature. If the rim of the pool is uneven or if it is built on a slight slope, build up a solid bank or retaining wall on the lower side. Although this sounds like a negative complication, it can have its bright side because the retaining wall could serve as a lovely poolside sitting area.

As the pool takes shape, check the edges with a carpenter's level strapped to a straight 2×4 that is slightly longer than the pool's width. A 4-foot level is easier to work with than a smaller one. You can rent a large transit level

▼ When a pond or pool is not level, problems occur. The liner may show above the waterline on the high side, or the water feature may overflow at the low point after a heavy rain.

from a local rental company. In the case of a large pool, you may have to put a grade stake in the middle of the excavated area to check the level of the pond rim. Put one end of the 2×4 on the grade stake and run the other end to every part of the pool edge. Check the level of the rim at every stage of excavation.

Any discrepancies in the level of the pool edge results in the liner showing unevenly. Poorly planned ponds can end up with the water level several inches below the rim at one end while overflowing at the other end. In a well-built pool, the liner will not be visible above the water level.

Note that a 2-percent grade in the bottom of the pool will make it easier to drain the pool for cleaning or repairs.

LEVELING LEDGES IN THE POND

Before installing the liner, check to be sure the excavation is level in all directions around the top edge. A slight variation in level of the ledges in the pond is less critical.

▼ If installing a rigid liner, check the level of the rim before you place the liner in the excavation and again as you backfill.

INSTALLING UNDERLAYMENT

Before putting down your pond liner, check the entire excavation for sharp protuberances, rocks, or roots. Next, put down a ½–1-inch layer of sand and smooth it out. Use a commercial underlayment to extend the lifetime of the liner that will be put down. The underlayment protects the liner from wear and tear, especially in sites with rocky soil or near tree roots.

▲ Use underlayment to cover the excavation's bottom and sides to help protect the liner.

Avoid using only newspaper or corrugated cardboard as underlayment. They disintegrate too quickly. You can, however, use carpet remnants, insulation felt, or flexible plastic foam. Nonwoven fabric underlays commonly called geotextile or landscape fabric are tough, reliable, and easy to use.

◀ Recycle old carpeting or rugs as an effective underlayment. Also place small pieces of carpet as a protective barrier between a flexible pond liner and hefty fountains or large rocks.

Whatever you use, place the underlay material over the entire surface of the hole. Butt the edges of the pieces together rather than overlapping them. Extend the underlay several inches beyond the edge of the pool so that the underlay does not get dislodged when you lay out the flexible pool liner. Carefully unroll the liner over the underlay. Adjust the liner as you go to allow it to sink into the excavation. Avoid disturbing the underlayment as you adjust the liner. It may take a team effort to smooth the liner while keeping the underlayment in place.

If you build your water feature in rock-free clay or loamy soil, you may not need to use underlayment. It still is a good idea to put down a thin layer of sand to smooth the soil. It need not be thick, just enough to provide a level surface at the bottom of the hole.

SMOOTH THE UNDERLAYMENT

Spread ½-1 inch of sand on all horizontal surfaces in the pool. This protects the liner from sharp objects in the excavation and cushions it from the weight of larger stones placed on top of the liner.

INSTALLING A RIGID POOL

Although it might appear easier to install a preformed pool than one with a flexible liner, that is often not the case. It is difficult to tailor the excavation exactly to the shape of the form. If the shape of the hole is a poor match to the liner, the whole pool may buckle and crack if the earth settles after rain or winter freezes. Another drawback to the preformed models is that they may not be deep enough to sustain hardy water plants that need a water depth of 18–24 inches. However, preformed rigid pools can be a good choice if installed properly.

Start the installation of a preformed pool by turning it upside down on the intended site. Mark the outline with rope, a garden hose, pegs, or lime. If it has two depths, invert it again and place it exactly over the first outline. Reach underneath and mark around the outline of the deeper section.

Next excavate the shapes to the same depths as the rigid pool itself, working 2–3 inches outside of the outlines and beyond the depths. When you have the excavation nearly done, put the rigid liner into the dug-out area, and then adjust the excavation to the rigid liner.

▼ **Use a spirit level on a long, straight board to check that the edge of the pond is level along its entire perimeter.**

When the excavation fits the liner, place 2 inches of sand in the bottom of the hole and rake the sand smooth. Place the rigid liner in the hole and check it with a carpenter's level across its width in several places. If it is not level, adjust the sand in the bottom of the hole until the rigid liner sits firmly with its rim level all around. Pay special attention to shelf areas that are shallower than the rest of the pool.

There will be gaps between the liner and the sides of the hole. Pour sand or fine soil into the gaps. Tamp it down well several times with a board or tool handle as you add more soil. Add a few inches of water to the pool and also pour some water into the gap to settle the pool and its surrounding soil. Take time to do this as success depends upon removing all air pockets as you backfill.

▲ As you backfill, tamp the soil firmly around the liner, and begin to fill the feature with water to help prevent the liner from popping out of the hole.

INSTALLING A FLEXIBLE LINER

When you are ready to install your flexible pond liner, roll the liner out loosely over the excavation. Having several people help at this stage will be a great advantage. Make sure that there is equal overlap on all sides. Anchor the corners of the liner temporarily with heavy rocks or other objects.

If you are constructing a large pool and thus have a large liner, follow the manufacturer's instructions on how to unfold the liner. The liner may need to be placed either at one end of the pool or at the center, depending upon how the supplier folded it.

Carefully walk all over the liner, helping it to move into place and mold itself to corners and curves. Begin to fill the pool with water. As it fills, pull and stretch the liner a bit to eliminate most of the wrinkles and folds. Move the corner weights and pinch the curves as the liner is pulled into the excavation by the weight of the water. Arrange the folds on the sides at curves and corners as unobtrusively as possible.

Once the pool has filled, smooth the overhang, trim it to about 1 foot in width, and pin down the overhang temporarily with 4-inch nails. Save some of the trimmings; the scraps prove handy as reinforcement under heavy

▼ Spread the liner over the excavation to make certain your size calculations were accurate. Don't worry about removing small folds at this stage.

objects or as mending patches. If you plan to put heavy objects such as fountains, pumps, or plant containers on the bottom, place cut-to-shape pieces of rigid plastic foam or a scrap of liner under them to protect the liner.

Bury the edges of both the liner and the underlay. Install coping or edging of an appropriate style to camouflage the liner. Be sure that the liner edges under the coping end with an upward turn. This keeps water from sneaking under the coping and out of the pond. If you use paving stones or flagstones as coping, extend them over the edge of the pool a bit to better disguise the liner. Plants that cascade over the edge of the pool offer another solution for hiding the liner and underlayment.

INSTALLING UNDERLAYMENT

Install underlayment over the sand layer. This fabric adds another layer of protection to prevent liner punctures. You can walk on the underlayment to conform it to the shape of the pond.

◀ Walk carefully within the site to push and pull the liner to conform to the shape of the excavation. Add rocks for a decorative touch or to hold the liner in place.

FILLING THE POOL

Once the liner has been installed and the pool completed, finish filling it with water. Let the water stand and mellow for several days. Use chloramine-removing chemicals that will work quickly and condition the water. Unless you use a chloramine remover, do not add fish for about two weeks. By waiting two weeks, you'll have a chance to fine-tune the pond and correct any problems before adding aquatic life.

Thirty to 60 days after installation, check the pH level with an easy-to-use kit you can purchase from a water garden nursery or retail

▼ **Filling the pool with water helps eliminate those final bends and awkward folds. Simply work to flatten them out as you fill the feature with water.**

At first, the water in the pool may turn murky. Do not empty it out and start over. It should clear itself in a few days.

outlet. If the pH is below 7, you will have an algae problem regardless of how many plants you install. Use manufactured products to alter the pH, following product label directions. Avoid changing the pH more than one point per day in an existing pond, especially if it contains fish, as they cannot tolerate rapid changes. Once plants and other aquatic life become established in the pond, they help regulate pH, too.

During the first two weeks, the water may develop a heavy algae bloom, often so severe that you can see no more than a few inches through the water. If this happens, don't become alarmed, and don't drain the pool. If the pH is around 7 to 10, the water should clear up once it strikes an ecological balance. Install submerged aquatic plants to remove the algae's nutrients and floating plants to shade the water. In time the water will clear up. Be patient and do not interfere with this natural process.

Algae are primitive green plants that grow wherever the right combination of water and sunlight are present. When the pool or pond is properly balanced, with the right mix of fish and plant life for the size of the water feature, the water will normally stay clear with little intervention. Periodically remove waste that collects on the bottom of the pool. Leaves and other debris that fall into the water rot and cause an imbalance if not removed on a regular basis.

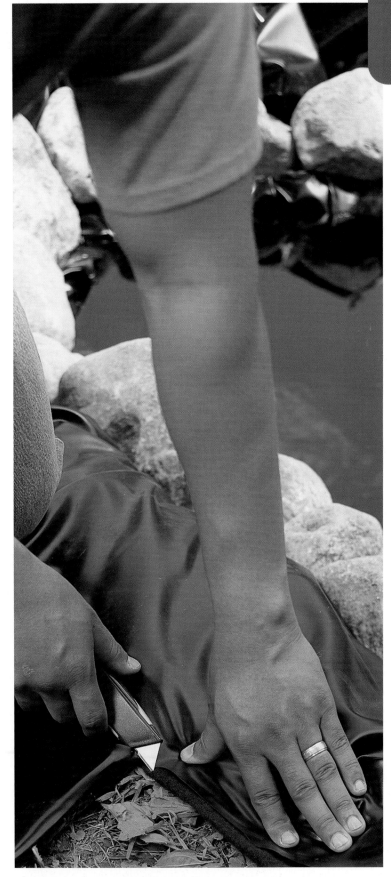

▼ Once the pool has filled and the coping is installed, trim the overlapping flap of excess pond liner.

FINISHING THE EDGES

The kind of edging or coping you use to finish the edges of your water feature depends upon the kind of use it will have. Is the edging strictly decorative? Will it have to stand up to foot traffic? Will the rim of the water feature be able to support the weight of the coping?

Some experts recommend that you install a concrete collar as the base for coping. Another way of accomplishing the same thing is to work ready-mix concrete into the top 4–6 inches of the soil around the edge of the water feature. If plants to accent the edge of the pool are part of your plan, you may prefer to install a few slabs of stone or rocks, and tuck the plants around the stone to emphasize the naturalized setting.

For a formal pool, bricks, slate, and paving stones accent the formality as will wooden decking in a geometric pattern. Adding a wall, both for sitting and for defining the area, can highlight overall formality. Paving stones of cast-concrete come in a wide range of colors, textures, and patterns. Some resemble brick. For a more permanent installation, set bricks, slate, or paving stones in mortar. If you are inexperienced in working with mortar, consider calling in a professional bricklayer or experienced landscape contractor.

Natural rocks, boulders, and pebbles are good choices for edging informal, free-form ponds. Artificial boulders cast from the real thing are lightweight and can substitute for

▶ Pool copings or edgings may be very informal as this one is with its rocks and stones from which low ground covers tumble over the edge of the garden pond.

natural ones. Partially bury large stones or boulders so that they appear as if they naturally occur there. Vary the sizes of the rocks and randomly place them to make the water feature look less contrived. Native grass edging around part of the pool adds to the created naturalness of the setting.

Fill the pond with water before placing any stone edging or trimming the liner to its final size. The liner must be free to shift slightly while the weight of the water pushes it into the contours of the pond. After the pond is full, place rocks and stones around the perimeter. Finish by trimming away excess liner 12 inches from the edge of the pool.

▶ Concrete provides a formal edging for this narrow pool from which umbrella palm (*Cyperus alternifolius*) grows.

FOUNTAINS

A fountain adds sound and movement to your water garden. Make certain your fountain blends into the design of your yard.

Avoid placing a fountain where water splashes on water lilies or other floating plants. The constant spray of water droplets rots the foliage, and moving water slows plant growth. Avoid installing a fountain where the spray overflows the pool draining water from it. The height of a fountain ideally is no more than half the diameter or width of the pool. Avoid installing a fountain where it is exposed to prevailing winds. Wind can blow the fountain spray out of a water feature. Turn off a fountain's pump prior to freezing weather or remove it. Store the pump and cords indoors in a sealed plastic bag.

If you live on a hilly site with a natural watercourse, you can have a fountain without a pump or electricity. Simply place the fountain partway down the slope and divert water through plastic piping to the fountain. Gravity creates the force to push water through the fountain. Place the fountain so that its water returns to the watercourse.

▲ Fountains come in many shapes and sizes. This ceramic pot with stones and a bubbler includes tiny planting pockets along the side.

Another way to get around the need for electrical connections is to buy a fountain and pump that operate on solar power. This option limits your choices to small fountains, but solar-powered fountains are easy to install and use.

◀ An outdoor showerhead is effectively used as a fountain in this garden pond, splashing the frog statuary, aerating the water for the koi, and adding pleasing sound to the site.

If child safety is a factor in developing your fountain, you have several good options. Install a fountain that drops its spray into a small underground reservoir. A bubbling fountain allows the water to seep into a tank beneath stones or a millstone. A wall fountain provides the sound and moving water without the dangers of deeper open water. A self-contained fountain feature in a container water garden provides less temptation to children than a larger pool of water.

▶ An attractive urn in the middle of a large concrete basin serves as the fountainhead for this water feature.

Choosing a Fountain

Look for a fountain that provides the precise effect you wish to create. Fountains run the gamut from the simplest little trickle, ideal for a patio, to rotating multijet displays including rainbows of underwater colored lights. For the average homeowner, the choice probably will lie somewhere in between.

Fountains come in such a wide variety of types and sizes that installation requirements almost must be considered on a unit by unit basis. Small fountains equipped with a pump and tubing need only be close to an electrical outlet, and fit into a small reservoir of water.

At the other end of the spectrum, you may have large garden statuary that already has necessary tubing in place, but needs to be connected to a pool and pump. A small submersible pump provides the necessary power to pump the water. Heavy statuary, however, should be placed on and mortared to a solid base. Construct the base with about 4 inches of concrete laid over 4 to 6 inches of compacted gravel. For a cleaner look stub in PVC piping for electrical and water lines as you pour the concrete. The statue may be in the pool or beside it, depending on which works best in the garden design.

◀ In a large pond, a central fountain can be quite handsome. However, water lilies and many other water plants do not thrive if they are constantly in the splash of the fountain.

Prepare the site for a wall fountain when the wall is being constructed. A wall fountain spouts water through a gargoyle or other artistic feature into a basin, then recirculates the water back to the spout. If the basin is big enough, conceal a small circulating pump at its bottom. Run the water piping behind the wall to the waterspout. If this simple solution doesn't work for your wall fountain you may need to build an underground reservoir to conceal the pump and piping.

▲ Install a wall fountain on a deck by mounting it on one of the deck post 4×4s. Raise the catch basin on bricks or drill through the decking to run the tubing to recirculate water.

◄ This ceramic statue of a small girl with a jug makes a quiet little fountain in a peaceful garden pool.

INSTALLING A FOUNTAIN

▲ **This urn fountain placed near the edge of the pool will be easy to access for maintenance.**

Installing a ready-made fountain is a simple task. Follow the instructions that come with the unit. Place the fountain in the pool in such a way that its spray falls within the confines of the pool. Use bricks or paving stones to raise the fountain base 2 inches or more from the bottom so that the pump does not pull in silt and debris. Make certain that the fountainhead sits at the surface of the water.

Place the fountain and pump near the edge of the pool to make periodic maintenance chores easier. Also place within reach of an existing GFCI-protected electrical outlet. If one is not handy, have a licensed electrician make the necessary modifications.

Use the recommended size of piping from the fountain to the pump in order to get maximum performance. Normally you should step up one size on the outlet. For example, if the outlet is $\frac{1}{4}$ inch in diameter, use $\frac{1}{2}$-inch tubing; on a $\frac{1}{2}$-inch outlet, use $\frac{3}{4}$-inch tubing. If you use undersize piping, the pump works less efficiently, and the fountain will not properly function. Place the pump close to the fountain rather than at the opposite side of the pool. This reduces the length of piping needed and increases the force of the fountain's spray.

The simplest fountainheads you can buy are made of molded plastic. They slide onto the top of most small- to medium-size submersible pumps. Brass jets are more durable than plastic and come in a wider variety. The holes in fountainheads may be fine or coarse. It's easier to clean debris from larger holes.

◀ Once aligned below the waterspout, the basin is ready for filling. Plug in the pump. Make any necessary adjustments to the basin, pump, hose, and spout to get the stream of water to fall at the right speed and location.

If the fountain is heavy, place a flat slab on the pool bottom in order to spread the weight and provide a sturdy base. Insert plastic matting, a piece of old carpeting, or extra layers of liner between the slab and the bottom of the pool to protect the liner.

▶ A heavy fountain such as this four-tier, free-form stone geyser requires a sturdy base to support it in the pond. Cushion the liner from the base to protect it from accidental punctures.

WATERFALLS

A good use for excavated soil from a garden pool is to build a berm with a watercourse and waterfall. A waterfall can be a bounding cascade or a trickling stream. Either way it expands the effects of your water garden. Power the waterfall with a recirculating submersible pump placed as close to the base of the water feature as possible for maximum power.

Fashion a formal waterfall into a style similar to a symmetrical formal garden. Build symmetry of materials and water into the design. If a nearby patio or terrace is constructed of bricks or of stone, build the waterfall of similar materials. If at all possible construct a formal waterfall at the same time as the hardscape for a precise match.

If you are fortunate enough to have a natural stream or brook through your property, adapt the stream to better fit your garden. You could change the streambed, put in a dam, add curves, or build a cascade. Check with your city or county zoning department to make certain any changes made are legal and up to code. If the site has a rocky ledge, use similar stone to create a naturalistic effect that blends into the existing topography. If you purchase stones and rocks, choose ones that blend well with each other. Select rocks and boulders of various sizes to maintain a naturalistic effect.

Another option for creating waterfalls is to use artificial rocks. They are cast in plastic or fiberglass, then colored to resemble natural stone. They are light and easy to handle, and can result in a handsome water feature.

Waterfalls come in all sizes and countless types. This tall cataract resembles mountain waterfalls. The rapids at its base are like a miniature mountain stream.

This small waterfall has a wide, quiet trickle such as you might find in a woodsy brook.

PREPARING THE SITE

To prepare a site for a waterfall or a series of cascading pools, waterproof the streambed or use preformed rigid plastic units.

If the property is nearly level, build a small hill or berm. Set up a sprinkler on the berm to settle the soil and make a stable base for your waterfall. Make this artificial hill appear as natural as possible. Gentle slopes look more natural. Cover the mound with a layer of topsoil. Then dig the waterway. Landscape the completed project with shrubs and perennials to accentuate the natural look.

If you waterproof the waterfall with flexible liner, use EPDM synthetic rubber. If you must piece it together, bond it with the recommended lap preparation, seam tape, and lap sealant. Alternatively make sure that each uphill piece overlaps the lower one by about 18 inches to prevent water leaking out through the seams. Hide the liner edges with rocks and plants. Pebbles and smooth stones in the channel add to the natural look.

If you use preformed plastic cascades, you can create a series of small waterfalls fairly easily, although they require careful anchoring. Install each unit level from side-to-side. If tipped slightly back, the small puddles of water remaining in the preformed cascade will make the water feature attractive even when the pump is turned off. Make certain that the water exiting over the lip of the waterfall does not flow back under the lip, undermining the waterfall.

Place the submersible pump as close as possible to the base of the cascade. Run piping from the base of the cascade to the top of the streambed. At the top the water can flow directly into the bed of the cascade, or can empty into a pool that leads to the waterfall.

As with waterfalls built with flexible liner, camouflage rigid-form cascade edges with rocks and plants. Position some of the surrounding plants so that they drape over the edge of the preformed cascade. This softens the harsh edges of the liner and creates a more natural look.

PONDS WITH WATERFALLS

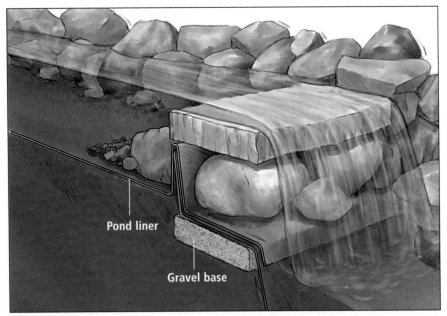

Pond liner

Gravel base

In single-step waterfalls, the pond becomes the holding area for water flowing over the waterfall. A smaller upper pool serves as the waterfall reservoir.

NATURAL RAPIDS

▲ In nature, water of a stream slices through the earth, eroding a bed for itself. Excavate the waterway deep enough for streams and waterfalls or rapids so that the water level will be slightly below grade. Edge the water feature with stones of various sizes placed in naturalistic ways.

◄ A sump containing a submersible pump recirculates the water from the base of a stream with waterfalls to the top of the hill. The pump can be pulled up to ground level for easy cleaning.

SELECTING A PUMP

P umps are available in many sizes and capacities. Choosing the right pump for fountains, waterfalls, or cascades can be mind-boggling. The pump must be powerful enough to send the water to the discharge point with enough force to make the water feature both beautiful and effective.

It pays to consult a dealer. Provide the supplier with the dimensions and volume of your pool and its fountain or cascade. Important to the choice of a pump are the height of the discharge outlet and the distance the water must be pumped. The higher the water must go, the less the volume of water the pump can move. Similarly, the longer the distance, the less the volume that can be pumped or the height to which it can be pumped. The maximum

distance that a pump can send water is called the head. Pump specifications found on the label should tell you its maximum head.

If the pump is to operate on house current, be sure that you have a licensed electrician install a ground fault circuit interrupter (GFCI) for safety's sake. Most communities require this type of circuit for outdoor installations. Make certain your electrical installation conforms to other local ordinances as well.

If the pump doesn't already have one, attach a physical water filter to the water intake. In its simplest form, this consists of a plastic canister wrapped with filter pad. Clean the filter by occasionally rinsing the filter pad in clear water or replace it. You can purchase filters and filter pads at water garden specialty stores.

CHOOSING A PUMP

Pipe to carry water to top of stream

Building a stream with a series of waterfalls or rapids ending in a pool or pond follows the same principles as building a pond. Excavate the streambed at least 8 inches deep. Place 1 inch of sand and underlayment in both the stream and the pond. Install the flexible liner in two pieces, one for the stream and one for the pond. Lap the end of the stream liner over the edge of the pond liner and seal the joint with the proper adhesive for the material. Place the pipe for recirculating water to the side of the pond and stream for easy access and maintenance.

◀ This is a bird's-eye view of an installed filter/skimmer combination with a pump for recirculating the water to the top of the waterfall.

◀ Insert a filter over the intake of the pump to extend the life of the pump and to prevent it from clogging with debris.

TUNING A WATERFALL

Each waterfall's or cascade's voice depends upon how it is constructed. The volume of water rushing or trickling along its channel affects its tone and degree of loudness. Alter the sound of the waterfall by changing the way the water flows over the edges of the drops or by altering the streambed itself.

▼ Changing the angle of the waterfall lip or adding stones to the lip will alter the sound of a waterfall. For an even flow across the falls, make certain the edge stone is level.

◄ Adding stones to the streambed or pond at the bottom of a waterfall will affect the sound the waterfall makes. Try single and multiple stones in various combinations until you are pleased with the sound.

◄ The sound of water flowing over rocks is an integral part of a Japanese garden.

If you want the water to flow over the edges in a single glistening sheet, add a slim lip of straight flagstone or a sheet of Plexiglas. This is an easy way to alter the sound and look of formal waterfalls and cascades.

You can change the sound of the waterfall by placing stones, bricks, or other heavy objects at the base where the water falls. Move these around until you are satisfied with the result. Another way to change the sound of a waterfall is to place stones or carve cuts into the lip of the fall. Adjust these—adding or subtracting stones or moving them around—until the sound pleases you.

You can tune your water feature by altering the volume of the flow. If the pump has no built-in volume adjustment, change the amount of water flowing through flexible tubing by installing a T-valve in the tubing near the pump outlet to recirculate the extra water back into the pond.

Finally, you can tune your cascade by creating rapids in the streambed. Add stones to the streambed—rounded stones provide a more natural look. Stones alter both the appearance and the sound of the water. Move them around until you have the sound you desire.

The Japanese go to great lengths to tune their water features. If you have visited Japanese gardens, you may have noticed the serene and peaceful moods created by cascades. Emulate the Japanese garden designers and patiently tune your waterfall or cascade.

RIVULETS, RILLS & RUNNELS

R ills, runnels, and rivulets are small streams used decoratively in water gardens. If it is geometric, following a precise line, right-angle turns, or repetitive curves that mirror each other, a rill will be right for a formal setting. If it follows a meandering path, it will be a fine addition to a naturalized water garden.

What is the difference between a stream and a rill? It's simply a matter of size. For the sake of discussion, a stream is more than 6 inches wide while a rill is less than 6 inches in width. Streams often are deeper than a couple of inches while rills are shallow. A rill can trickle over the edge of miniature cliffs as it returns to a pool. It represents a mountain with a cataract spilling over the edge.

Think of rills as streams and waterfalls on a tiny scale. They are ideal for limited spaces such as the corner of a patio or on a porch. Use a rill

▶ Stones in various sizes and placements alter the water flow in this stream, making it splash and gurgle with a lively sound.

▲ Water splashing down the slope and around the stones of this rivulet is a treat to both eyes and ears.

in an indoor garden where the rill provides the attraction of moving water without large pools of water.

If you plan to build a brick or stone patio, consider including a formal rill in the plan by building channels into the patio. Here, water can slowly flow along a geometric streambed, adding the pleasant sight of water to an otherwise dry setting. If children are often in this area, they can safely play by a rill.

▶ This runnel, lined with smooth, rounded river rocks, carries water from one level to another in a charming manner.

PREPARING THE SITE

The site where you plan to construct a rill needs a slight grade to it. Use a carpenter's level to assess the slope. If you want the rill to become part of a patio, for instance, build the grade into the patio, thus assuring that the rill will flow.

If you build a rill into a patio, line the bed with flexible EPDM liner, put down a layer of concrete, edge with a layer of exterior brick, and top with paving stones. Install flexible tubing to recirculate the water underneath the bricks or pavers to the side of the rill.

For a naturalized rill, take cues from nature, preparing a bed that meanders down a slope, and flows around obstructions such as boulders. Prepare the bed for a rill just as you would for a larger stream. Dig it out and tamp the soil to

compact it. Use flexible EPDM liner to waterproof the bed. If you have to piece the liner, either overlap the upper over the lower piece by 18 inches or use a bonding kit made for EPDM.

Conceal the edges of the rill. Use rocks similar to those in your region to emphasize the naturalness of the water feature. If these are ledge rocks, arrange them in the same way as they are in nature. Allow the rocks to slightly overlap the edge of the rill to help hide the liner. If you use rounded rocks, choose several sizes and arrange them as they might be near a rocky stream. Partially bury larger rocks to give them a more natural look. Combine plants with the stone, choosing those that creep over the edge of the liner.

▼ **This runnel proceeds from fountain and waterfall to slide between broad steps on a bed of smooth rounded stones.**

◀ Artistic, naturalistic rock placement makes the difference between a water feature that looks contrived and one that appears created by nature.

◀ A snorkel for a rivulet is installed with the flexible liner. The snorkel houses the pump that recirculates the water back to the top of the stream or rivulet.

SELECTING A PUMP

A pump adds motion to your water feature. Study the lift and volume requirements of your water feature. Match those needs to a good quality pump. It is better to get a pump that is larger than the minimum you need for lift rather than one that is scarcely adequate. Such factors as a clogged intake filter restrict the flow of water and limit the effectiveness of the pump. By selecting a larger pump your water feature will continue to have adequate flow under less than ideal circumstances.

Submersible garden pumps are easier to install than external ones. External pumps are usually installed in waterproof housing to prolong their life and reduce noise. While submersibles are a better choice for most water gardens, complex water features may call for an external pump if greater head pressure is needed for long-distance runs or filtration.

Electricity and water are dangerous together. Have a licensed electrician install necessary outlets and substation boxes. Avoid using extension cords to power a water garden pump.

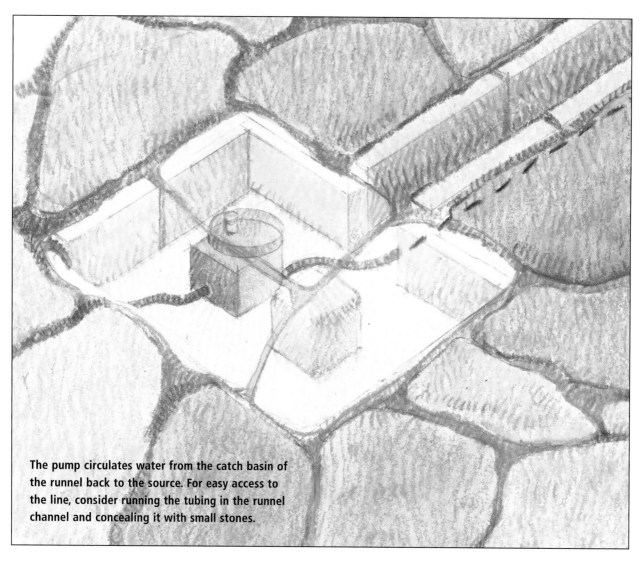

The pump circulates water from the catch basin of the runnel back to the source. For easy access to the line, consider running the tubing in the runnel channel and concealing it with small stones.

▲ A small rill runs in a narrow channel between steps that descend to a round formal pool, making the last jump as a trickling waterfall that adds sound to the peaceful sight.

Safety should be your first consideration whenever you add electricity to your garden.

Solar pumps have come of age in recent years. Today's solar pumps can operate even on cloudy days. Although they are a bit pricey compared to submersible pumps, consider that they do not need electrical connections, a cost savings in construction and in usage.

▶ Rills run on both sides of the palm-planted island bed, leading from a formal pool planted with umbrella palms.

RAIN GARDENS

Comparative newcomers to the garden scene are rain gardens. They are wetland gardens created in areas plagued with standing water, runoff, or erosion. Rain gardens eliminate the need for more expensive solutions such as regrading the property or installing drain tiles.

Rain gardens solve these problems in natural ways. The plants in a rain garden slow down the water and increase the infiltration of the water into the soil, just as forests and prairies do in nature. Rain gardens conserve water by replenishing the water in the soil, a good solution for drought regions. They also diminish flooding and lessen runoff pollution to streams and lakes.

Native plants are often planted in rain gardens, continuing the natural theme. Most rain gardens have three zones. The upper zone nearest the source of the runoff is the driest and can be planted with most native shrubs, trees, and perennials. A middle zone, where the soil is usually moist but may have drought periods, is a good site for plants such as cardinal flower, black-eyed Susan, sweetbay magnolia, and river birch. The lowest part of the rain garden is where the soil is the moistest even though it, too, may have dry periods. Plants for this area include swamp milkweed, sedges, and New England aster. Which plants are used and the size and shape of the garden are derived from the specifics of the site.

▶ This site is a likely candidate for a makeover into a rain garden. As is, the soil turns mucky when wet and erodes when dry.

Every rain garden has a shallow depression where the runoff first collects. Amend the soil in the bottom of this saucer with organic matter, gravel, and mulch to improve its drainage. Soils with a pH of 5.5 to 6.5 have the best capacity for the kind of biochemical reactions that convert pollutants to harmless substances. For maximum effect, consider amending the soil to achieve a pH between these levels.

▼ The site on page 126 was converted into a rain garden by planting hibiscus, cannas, calla lilies, and maiden grass. All tolerate wet sites, but thrive in drier soils too.

Begin the construction of your rain garden by building a small berm to retain water. Amend the soil with organic matter in the planting bed before planting.

PREPARING THE SITE

Spring is a good time to create a rain garden. Before starting, take the time to study what happens during a downpour. Where does the water come from? Where does it go? What area is involved? How long does the water stand after the rain stops? Answer these questions before you delineate the rain garden area.

Locate the rain garden in sun to partial shade just downhill from the source of water, but at least 20 feet away from the foundation of the house. The larger the volume of water coming from the source, the larger the proposed rain garden should be. Make the rain garden approximately twice as long as it is wide, with the width measured from uphill to down.

USE RAINFALL RUNOFF ON SITE

Direct water to planting beds. Make sure the soil is well-aerated and drains well.

Position the rain garden so that it is roughly perpendicular to the source of runoff water.

Mark the outline of the garden with a garden hose, rope, or lime. Eliminate grass and other plants within the area by spraying with glyphosate herbicide or put black plastic over the area for several weeks until the plants die. Start digging on the uphill side of the rain garden and use that soil to build a berm along the lower side. A curved berm will be more attractive and look more natural than a straight one. Level the area between the upper edge of the rain garden and the berm. Judging level on a slope can be deceiving to the eye; use a carpenter's level to be certain.

▲ **This rain garden is constructed to hold rainfall and runoff, allowing it to seep slowly into the earth, conserving water and adding to the water table.**

Tamp down the soil in the berm. Build the crest of the berm at least a foot wide to create a natural appearance, and gently slope the sides to prevent erosion. Until the berm is permanently landscaped, plant annual ryegrass and mulch it with straw to prevent erosion. If the water source is from a downspout, put an extension on the downspout or make a grassy swale to lead the water into the rain garden.

COMPLETING THE RAIN GARDEN

Add compost to improve the soil in the rain garden. Compost greatly improves the quality and texture of the soil, allowing water to seep in faster. If the soil is dense clay, you may want to also add gravel for better infiltration of water. Put down a 2- to 4-inch layer of mulch on top of the soil. Mulch acts as a sponge to absorb water, allowing it to sink into the soil more gently. Mulch also encourages biological activity that filters pollutants and converts them into harmless substances.

Although you may be tempted to plant the rain garden with a wildflower seed mix, don't. It is difficult to protect the seeds from the elements long enough for them to become established. It's far better to transplant pots of plants with established root systems. Transplants adjust to the new setting faster and more quickly fulfill their role of slowing down and absorbing the runoff water. If you already grow some of the plants adapted to a rain garden, use this as an excuse to divide and replant them.

For areas in the rain garden where the soil stays moist or wet for long periods, rushes and reeds are good choices. If the area has standing water for lengthy periods, pickerel weed and arrowhead will thrive. Plants for the rest of the rain garden include sedges, swamp milkweed, New England aster, Joe-Pye weed, hibiscus, cardinal flower, ironweed, and black-eyed Susan. Winter-hardy natives make your rain garden a beautiful water feature. Install a bench or two and you will have a lovely place where you can contemplate the good things in life.

▼ Swamp mallow, also known as hardy hibiscus, *(H. moscheutos)* makes a showy, perennial addition to a rain garden.

This rain garden has handsome plantings of Siberian iris, junipers, and barberries that will thrive under the alternating wet and dry conditions that may exist in a swale.

BOG GARDENS

Y ou may have a potential site for a bog garden in a low, damp place on your property; simply exaggerate the conditions that already are present. A bog may be separate or may be an extension of a pond. Bogs host a number of plants that thrive in damp soil that other plants can't tolerate.

Some ferns are good subjects for bog gardens, including ostrich fern, royal fern, and sensitive fern. Cardinal flower, meadowsweet, and daylily thrive in damp soil as do astilbe,

▲ **Plants that are best for a bog garden are those that thrive in moist to wet soil. Here yellow primrose *(Primula prolifera)* combines with white-flowered skunk cabbage *(Lysichiton camtschatcensis)* to make a stunning display of textures and colors.**

hosta, and Japanese iris. Reeds and sedges offer textural variety to the bog. When planted with care and an eye for design, a bog garden is appealing and beautiful.

Whether you create a bog garden in association with a pool or by itself, the process

is the same. The soil must constantly be moist, yet water should slowly drain out of the area or it will stagnate. When the bog garden has flexible liner as its base, overflow the bog periodically to keep water fresh or maintain uniform moisture with automatic sprinklers.

Bog gardens attract a wide variety of beneficial insects and butterflies. But remember that butterflies and moths are the grownup versions of caterpillars that feed on plants. If you want butterflies, expect to share some of your plants with the caterpillars.

▲ A variety of plants including rushes, sedges, some ferns, some hardy hibiscuses, and many others will thrive under boggy conditions. In this planting, creagh fern, calla lily, and primroses provide a striking mix of plant forms.

PREPARING THE SITE

Water

Soil

Pea gravel

Sand

I f you want to grow a wide variety of plants in your bog garden, choose a sunny site. Moist soil in the bog allows some shade plants to grow well in sun—extra moisture makes the difference.

Outline the site for your bog garden with garden hose or rope. An oval or round site looks more natural and conserves moisture better than a long thin bog garden. Dig the bog about 18 inches deep in its center. Slope the sides to the edge.

Put flexible liner down in the excavation site. Underlayment is unnecessary since an occasional hole in the liner is needed for

▲ Constructing an artificial bog garden involves digging the site and laying down soil on top of flexible liner, and then selecting plants that will thrive in these conditions.

drainage. With a bog garden you need not worry about finishing the edges either. Trim the excess liner to just below the surrounding soil level. Maintain a 3-inch layer of water over the soil in the bog. Stock it with mosquito fish to prevent creation of mosquito breeding grounds.

To make periodic watering easier, place a soaker hose at the bottom of the dug-out area with the connecting end of the hose up and outside the edge of the bog garden. Or use perforated rigid piping with a hose attached. Place the hose end with connectors on the slope and over the edge of the garden. This allows you to attach a garden hose and water the bog garden when it needs it.

Put several inches of pea gravel down on the bottom of the liner. Rake the gravel smooth. Fill the bog garden with soil, firming it as you go. Avoid using high levels of organic matter which can decay, creating an odor problem and attracting bugs and flies.

▼ Irises, cattails, and cotton grass (*Eriophorum angustifolium*) thrive in the boggy conditions of this site that blends with its surroundings.

COMPLETING THE BOG GARDEN

▶ This bog garden is a winner with its beautiful selection of plants that have interesting textures and growth forms as well as colorful flowers. Bold hosta foliage in the foreground contrasts with pink and white primroses and the linear foliage of irises.

Once the bog garden is completed, fill it with water. Add water until you see the soil surface flooding. During dry spells, add water weekly or even more often as the soil dries.

An occasional boulder or stone adds an interesting note to the garden and can delineate the edge of the garden. Add a bench or other seating to provide a place where you can sit and contemplate the scene.

Plant the bog garden densely with patches of perennials in groupings of three, five, or seven—odd-number groupings are aesthetically more pleasing. Informal plantings look natural and spread as they become established.

Red- or yellow-twig dogwoods provide decorative edging to the bog garden. Cut them back to the ground just before they come into leaf in order to keep the twigs bright. Alders thrive in a boggy site. Cut them back hard to

▶ **This bog garden features a number of attractive ornamentals including irises and primroses.**

keep them bushy. Yellow-flag irises grow well in wet soils, so well that in some areas they are banned. Choose from ones with variegated foliage or plain green.

Cattails and reeds add strong vertical strokes to the garden. Sedges come in many sizes and tints. Watermint, a low ground cover, adds fragrance and bears pink flowers. Be prepared to regularly pull it as it spreads.

It may be difficult to reach some of the plants to do needed maintenance. An easy, inexpensive solution is to use squares of plywood as temporary stepping-stones. Permanent stepping-stones can be both decorative and useful. In large bog gardens, install permanent paths of shredded hardwood bark mulch to allow passage to various parts of the garden.

◀ **A bog garden that merges into a garden pool features round stepping-stones that invite the visitor to follow the pathway across the marshy ground.**

DRY CREEKS

When a stream or pool is not feasible, a dry streambed offers the illusion of a water feature. A dry creek suggests moving water even though it carries none except, perhaps, during a rainstorm. Smooth stones and rounded gravel add to the illusion of moving water when placed in the dry creek streambed. A few carefully placed larger stones serve as an attractive focal point and double as streamside seating.

A dry creek can channel storm water into garden beds and borders, and thus aid drought areas when summer storms hit. Increase the illusion of moving water in a dry streambed by planting reedlike plants along the edges. Plant a line of low-growing, mat-forming plants along the contours of the dry streambed to provide a sense of motion. Add a few large flat stepping-stones for crossing the dry streambed to enhance the illusion.

If your site is flat, take inspiration from Japanese gardens which conjure up water in a number of ways. They use dry water features to represent streams, lakes, and seas. With gravel raked into ripples along the edges and around stone islands, a feature can remind you of a real river even though no water runs through it.

◄ **Flowering annuals lead your eye along the length of the border of this dry creek that has a bed of smooth gray stones resembling flowing water.**

◀ Bluish-gray stones tumble down the center of the dry creek while larger irregular stones and rocks mark the banks.

▶ Smooth rounded stones have become a signature for dry creeks. They are reminiscent of natural creeks and streams. Desert plants edge the banks of this dry creek which is in an arid region.

PREPARING THE SITE

DRY CREEK BED

If the bed will not carry water runoff, simply cover the area with landscape fabric, and then add a 1-inch layer of pea gravel or gravel and sand mix.

A dry creek should look like a stream that has run out of water. Such streambeds are common in hilly country where dry creeks naturally drain the hillsides during stormy spells, but are dry throughout the rest of the year. Study the lay of your land, noting where water flows after a rainstorm. Create a dry creek along the route rainfall runoff naturally flows. You may observe a natural channel that can be enhanced by widening and deepening the course.

If you create an alternate course for the dry creek, test it with water before proceeding any further. Dig the new course in such a way that it is attractive and yet channels rainwater. If your property is flat, you can develop either a dry streambed or dry pond with appropriate stones and pebbles.

The first step is to outline the area where the dry bed will go with either rope or garden hose. If the dry streambed or dry pond holds no

DRY CREEK CONSTRUCTION

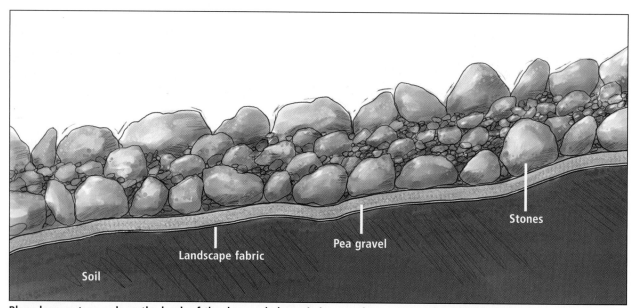

Stones

Pea gravel

Landscape fabric

Soil

Place larger stones along the bank of the dry creek, but mix in some large stones throughout the middle of the bed as well. Don't keep an even width. Streams tend to be wider on curves and narrower where they run relatively straight.

water, even after a rainstorm, you need only lay down nonwoven landscape fabric called geotextile on the bed. The fabric makes a good weedproof base for the pebbles, rocks, and gravel. If, on the other hand, the dry creek will carry storm water at times, direct the water to a planted area that can absorb it. Then put down underlayment topped by flexible pond liner, just as you would for a water feature.

Placement of rounded stones and pebbles creates the effect of rushing water. Take your time in arranging the stones. Oval stones and pebbles placed lengthwise in the streambed are most effective in creating the illusion of moving water. Random placement of stones distracts from the illusion. Adding a row of contrasting stones at both edges of the creek enhances the illusory effect.

▲ Naturalized plantings plus well-arranged stones and a supported stone slab bridge all add up to a magnificent example of a dry creek garden.

COMPLETING A DRY CREEK

If the base of your dry creek is landscape fabric, add a 1- to 2-inch layer of clean gravel or sand over the fabric before placing pebbles and rocks. The pebbles sink slightly into the sand, providing a more natural appearance. If you use flexible liner as the base of the feature, position stones and pebbles first; then finish with clean gravel that sinks into pockets between the stones.

If you use boulders or bigger stones along the banks of the dry creek, bury the bottom ⅓ to ⅔ in the soil. This makes them seem as though they have been there for years.

Planting is the final touch to finish the dry creek. The choices of plants are countless. Much depends upon your personal taste and your specific region. Use plants native to the area to make the feature look more natural. Ornamental grasses are a good choice if the feature is in the sun. Try Korean feather reedgrass, placing three groupings of five plants scattered along the streambed if it is fairly long. Blue fescue is a good choice if the dry streambed is small. Edge the banks with green mats of rock rose. For a shady site, sedges offer a grasslike appearance. Use astilbe, dianthus, and coralbells for a woodland effect. Small shrubs and trees add to the overall beauty of the setting.

◀ **Irises and other ornamentals with vertical growth patterns define the meandering path of this handsome dry creek.**

Japanese gardens often include dry creeks as well as dry lakes and even dry oceans. They are decorative and symbolic of features in the real and larger world.

Indoor Water Features

The appeal of indoor water features is hard to resist. Yet indoor water features present particular challenges and hazards.

Check with a contractor if in doubt about the weight-bearing capacity of a floor where you want to put a heavy containerized water garden. Water can escape through tiny holes, harming or rotting flooring. Floor coverings near the water garden should be water-resistant. Occasional spills or leaks are certain to happen.

A glassed-in sunporch with a poured concrete floor is an ideal location for an indoor water garden. Here, potential water leaks are not as damaging and weight-bearing capacity is not an issue. Most aquatic plants require bright light for good growth. A small pool in the light, bright space could be the perfect setting for a few aquatic plants.

Create the illusion of a jungle pool by grouping houseplants around the sides. Most houseplants are native to tropical or semitropical regions so they naturally provide a lush tropical feel to the water feature. The plants appreciate the high humidity

◀ **Adding stones to the base of an indoor fountain gives it a more naturalistic appearance and may help hide the pump and electrical cord.**

provided by evaporation from the water garden. Place plants in individual catch basins or saucers to prevent water staining on the flooring. Group larger pots with taller plants toward the rear of the site and smaller ones in the front. Plants that drape over the edges of the pots are best for the front of the grouping, softening the rims of the containers. Be sure to use plants with similar light requirements. If your site has plenty of light, you'll have more options to choose from. However, even in dim light, a variety of plant forms, colors, and textures are available to complement your indoor water garden.

▼ **Water lettuce and water hyacinth make an interesting indoor water garden when kept in a roomy bowl set in bright light. This attractive combination is small enough to function as a centerpiece for a dinner table.**

▲ Rectangular receptacles of water superimposed on one another create a dramatic fountain flanking this stairway.

▲ A self-contained fountain, installed easily from a kit, makes a welcoming feature in an entryway. This one snaps together with two pieces plus a pump and pump cover.

All sorts of ready-made water features are available for indoor usage. Electrical connections and water piping are built into them. Place one on a sturdy table or ledge, add water, plug it in, and it's ready to go.

Another easy way to have an indoor water feature is to use a large plastic pot (with no drainage holes), galvanized washtub, half whiskey barrel with liner, or other large container as the basis for your water garden.

A small bubbling fountain will oxygenate the water yet won't create enough water current to hinder plant growth. Small floating plants such as water lettuce and water hyacinth thrive in such a setting.

◀ This raised indoor water feature includes a lion's head wall fountain and is surrounded by attractive containerized plants.

▼ Set up a small rigid pool indoors and complete the lively scene by adding a water lettuce plant or two, a couple of goldfish, and a few houseplants.

Look for wall fountains that are already fitted with plumbing and small pumps. Even a small one adds the sound and sight of moving water. If plants or fish are absent from the fountain, add chlorine to the water to prevent the growth of pump-clogging algae.

Consider using a large aquarium as an indoor water feature. Already thoroughly waterproof, an aquarium fits on a shelf or table and has potential as a water feature that includes both aquatic plants and fish. Aquarium-sized pumps and filters are available at pet shops. An aquarium offers an opportunity that most other containerized water gardens do not: You can see through the sides of the garden and observe both plant and animal life.

PREPARING THE SITE

You can easily prepare simple indoor water features. If using a container for the water feature, avoid using one made of lead or copper. These metals corrode when exposed to fertilizers. If you plan to grow emerging or floating plants, first put down a layer of pea gravel or coarse sand. Add a pinch of charcoal powder or small piece of charcoal to keep the water from becoming foul. Prepare a dilute water and fertilizer solution. Use the water-soluble fertilizer at a rate that is only ⅕ to ½ the recommended rate. Add this to the container. Finally, fill the container to within ½ to 1 inch of the rim. Leave the plants in pots or transplant them into the coarse medium. You can raise the levels of the pots with bricks if need be.

When installing a ready-made water feature kit, choose the site with care. Avoid placing the feature near items that clash with it. If the feature is tall, it could sit directly on the floor or on a low pedestal. Lower profile water feature kits are ideal for tables or taller pedestals.

▼ **Low walls contain the water of this indoor water feature. Statuary, stones, and begonias add interest.**

▶ This handsome ceramic fish wall fountain is the centerpiece of this indoor water feature. A basket of lavender completes the scene.

If you choose to grow fish and plants in an aquarium, purchase aquarium gravel and put down a 2- to 4-inch layer in the bottom of the aquarium. Include a few small bits of charcoal to keep the water fresh. Add variety by pushing the gravel into low mounds and valleys. Use decorative rocks to keep plant roots in place where you want them.

Hire a professional contractor to install a water garden over hardwood floors or on subflooring in a foyer or den. Use a 4- to 6-inch-wide retaining wall of finished lumber to hold a flexible liner. Or choose a small preformed pool. Decorate the pool with a fountain or waterfall. As little as 4 inches of potting soil will be enough to allow plants to grow and thrive around the pool. Leave plants in their pots and plunge them into the soil or transplant them directly into the soil. Apply organic mulch for a groomed look.

Singly or in groupings, plants add a softening touch to indoor water features. Indulge your own particular tastes. If it's orchids you love, buy a bunch of them and include them in or around your water feature.

▲ What makes a freestanding fountain appealing? For starters, it's easy to install, clean, and maintain. The slate in this fountain pairs nicely with the slate-look tile flooring in this entry hall.

CHAPTER HIGHLIGHTS

This chapter tells you how to enhance
your water feature, making it more
enjoyable by adding useful and
decorative things such as seating,
paths, bridges, decks, lighting,
fountains, art, and sculpture.

ENHANCING WATER GARDENS

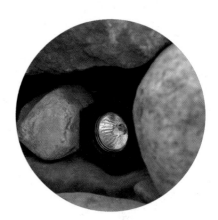

Once you have finished the construction of the water feature and put together all of its necessary components, all that's left is to add frosting to the cake. The frosting in this case includes all of those items that make the water garden more beautiful, more comfortable, and easier to fit into your lifestyle.

A well-designed water garden is a peaceful paradise where relaxation is more serene and enjoyable. Create honest relationships between the water feature and other elements of the garden. Whether your chosen style is formal, informal, or eclectic doesn't matter as much as how well the different parts of the garden fit together.

This chapter suggests water-feature enhancements you might want to explore. Many of these garden accessories are available ready-made or in kits.

To guide your decision, answer the following:

■ What views do you want to emphasize?

■ Where is a comfortable, convenient place for seating?

■ Where would paths encourage a scenic walk?

■ What pathways or access points would make garden maintenance easier?

SEATING

▲ **Rustic chairs fit in well with the informal design of this home with its naturalistic waterfall.**

When you've decided where you would like to sit, dine, and stroll through the garden, consider the table and seating style that blends well with your existing home and garden. While a simple cedar bench might suit an informal site, a more elegant wrought-iron bench works better in a formal garden.

Formal settings call for symmetrical design and arrangement. Balance and finely finished furniture suits formal settings far better than bentwood, twig, or Adirondack chairs. Wrought-iron chairs and a glass-top wrought-iron table add elegance.

Classic outdoor furniture designs that bring to mind the splendors of significant design eras—Empire, Victorian, Neoclassical— enhance the balance and constructed qualities of a

▶ **This simple wooden chair complements the Oriental flavor of this water garden.**

formal garden. Cushions make these pieces more comfortable. Provide shelter for the cushions during rainy weather in a chest that is lidded and waterproof. Use the chest as extra seating and as shelter for perishable items.

Formal carved teak benches resemble those used to accent Victorian gardens. The handsome benches fit formal water gardens and properties. They also work well in informal settings, adding a rich note to the property.

Informal settings are more common and, for most people, easier to work with. Many items can work well as seating near an informal water garden. Place a boulder of suitable size to capture a view across a garden pool or a view that includes a fountain or waterfall. Ideally, the

flat-top boulder should be wide enough to seat two. Sink ⅓ to ½ of its height into the ground and it will look as if the glaciers had dropped it there thousands of years ago.

Wooden benches of many styles can enhance water gardens of any scale. Plastic furniture includes a number of designs appropriate for gardens. Don't forget concrete benches and tables that might fit into either formal or informal water gardens.

▲ A bench in a shady spot by a garden pool will be difficult to resist on a hot summer day.

PATHS AND PAVERS

Paths and stepping-stones point the way to go. They may lead you from patio to water garden, from back door to a sitting area by a fountain or waterfall, or to the rear of a water feature where you can perform needed maintenance. On large properties, paths may lead you on a scenic tour from a vista across a garden pool, through a bit of woodland, and over a small bridge that spans the garden pool.

The simplest path is a grassy way that meanders between garden beds and borders. Mowing is the only maintenance needed. Soft grass is inviting to the bare feet of summer. Edge the beds around the pool and along the path to provide definition and add formality.

Paving stones, flat pieces of slate, or other flat rocks that are about an inch thick can be laid on the sod to create a stepping-stone pathway. Cut and remove the sod directly under the stones so that the stones sit slightly below grade, making mowing easier.

If the area is mostly shaded, use landscape fabric to create a simple path. Shear grass and weeds to the ground with a weed eater, and then put down a layer of the fabric. Finish the path with 2 to 4 inches of shredded bark or pea gravel. Rake periodically to keep the path smooth. Add more mulch or pea gravel if the layer becomes too thin.

◄ Space stones along a stepping-stone path to invite a slow walking pace. Soften the effect of stones by planting a creeping ground cover between the individual stones.

Patterned, colored, or textured poured concrete provides a wonderful surface for walking. Such a path will last many years. Choose from handsome patterns resembling slate, brick, or sandstone. Use patterned concrete forms and bagged concrete mix to create your own design at a fraction of the cost of professional hardscape installation.

Whatever pathway you choose to build, match it to the water garden and property as a whole in style and mood. Most of all, make sure that the resulting path pleases you.

◄ Stepping-stones that bridge a garden stream offer a striking alternative to the more formal stone patio.

► Bricks or pavers offer another way to construct a pathway to and around the water garden.

BRIDGES AND PIERS

A bridge can be the crowning glory of a garden pool. A bridge is a good connector for paths and different parts of the garden. For most water features, a bridge with a simple design built close to the water works well. Build the bridge in scale with the pool. For a small water feature, a simple large stepping-stone that spans a narrow place would be good.

An arched bridge has gentle curves that combine well with ponds. While many Japanese gardens have a large-scale drum bridge that leads to an island, a smaller curved bridge designed for a home water feature has the essence, if not the grandeur, of a drum bridge.

Another Japanese garden feature that can be useful in water gardens is the crooked bridge that consists of straight spans set at right angles to each other. A crooked bridge is, according to Japanese tradition, the way to get rid of evil spirits since the bad spirits can not turn corners.

You can make a simple rustic bridge of stained and waterproofed 2×6 redwood or cedar lumber laid across a narrow waterway. Place the ends of the lumber on flat paving stones, cinder blocks, or concrete bases. You may add

▼ A small arched bridge spans a water garden, inviting you to walk across into another part of the landscape.

Even home gardens can include a Japanese crooked bridge in the water garden. Such a bridge is reputed to repel evil spirits that are unable to make right-angle turns.

handrails as a safety factor, and they can add a decorative quality to the bridge. Some local building codes may require installation of handrails.

A pier that resembles a functional boat dock is another means of making your water garden imply that it is part of a lake or river rather than simply a small pond. Constructing a pier is similar to constructing a deck. For the best effect, cantilever the pier slightly over the water—it will look more natural. A pier creates a grand spot for a picnic or a cool drink. Equally good for feeding fish and for taking a rest from the busy world, a pier might be a good addition to your water garden.

▶ A formal bridge with finials enhances the water feature of this home.

DECKS

▲ **Limestone slab steps that lead down to the garden pond can serve as a fish-feeding site or as extra seating.**

A deck adds a finished look to the water garden while providing a good spot for viewing the pool or pond. It's a great place for relaxing and enjoying a simple snack or a sumptuous meal next to your water feature. Where the land is uneven, a deck offers a flat surface for tables, benches, and chairs. If you plan a deck so that a stream emerges from underneath, you will find that the hollow area below the deck enhances the sound.

Wood offers a warm, attractive surface for bare feet in spring and summer. Waterproof and stain it to blend with the surroundings. Be careful using stains and waterproofing materials around a pool that includes fish. Some ingredients are dangerous to fish and other water life.

Plastic lumber, made of recycled materials, is worth considering for its longevity and good looks. Plastic lumber is easy to work with. Look for plastic lumber with a textured surface. It will not be slippery when wet.

▼ Through careful and artistic design, this deck and bench have become a vital accompaniment to this water feature.

Designs for decks range widely in size and style. They need not be rectangular—a deck can sweep in an arc around the water. From a structural point of view, a deck should have sound footings and a strong foundation. Have a contractor or carpenter install the deck to your design if you have little carpentry experience. It's important that the construction have joists and uprights strong enough to support more than the expected weight.

Once the base and supports for the deck are built, install planking in line with the edges or diagonally. The latter gives a custom look to an otherwise ordinary deck. If you lay the planking in square sections perpendicular to each other, the deck forms an attractive basket-weave look.

Create garden paths that lead people to the deck. If small children or elderly people often will be enjoying the water garden, construct a sturdy railing for the deck as a safety feature.

▲ This elegant deck is more formal yet greatly enhances the rockwork and naturalistic plantings of the nearby stream.

LIGHTING

Lights in a water garden can transform the area into a magical oasis that can be enjoyed in the evening. Focus lighting on a fountain or waterfall to add a dramatic quality that is unimaginable during daylight hours.

▲ Strategically placed lighting enhances the beauty of this garden pool with its lovely fountains and rock sculptures.

Lighting can brighten paths, decks, bridges, and water features, making the garden a pleasurable and safe place for a walk, a meal, or simply enjoying your outdoor living space after the sun goes down. Lighting attached to infrared motion detectors increases home security as it deters intruders. Shine spotlights up into trees for a leafy green glow. Create pools of light along pathways and in sitting areas. Make certain that the light is bright enough to guide you but not glaring.

◄ Soft lighting brings out the warmth and the drama of this pool with its ram's head wall fountain.

If the garden lighting is part of the household electrical system, call in an electrician to install safe wiring and outlets. Have the electrician set up the system so that you can use low-voltage lighting. Once that is done, choose a combination of floodlights and spotlights to create the impact you want.

Another option is solar-power lighting. It requires no electrician to install because it derives its energy from the sun. For most systems, five to eight hours of sunlight per day is sufficient. As a result, the solar panels can not be in shady places if they are to be efficient. The energy is stored in rechargeable internal batteries. Further, the wiring does not have to be put underground. With solar-power lighting, sensors turn the lights on at dusk and off at dawn. You can purchase solar-power lights with built-in motion sensors that turn the lights on and off automatically when you walk by, conserving power. Some solar-power lights come with stakes that you push into the ground at the base of plants or paths you want to light. Other models attach directly to the sides of buildings or trees.

▲ Well-placed night lighting lends a glowing quality to water features such as these fountains. Try light bulbs of various colors to achieve the effect you desire.

FOUNTAINS

▼ **Fountains can be added after the original water feature is complete. This is one example of the many fountainheads that are available from water garden supply centers.**

If you already have a water garden, you may want to enhance your existing garden pool with a beautiful fountain. In this case, your choices are limited unless you reconstruct part of the pool to add plumbing and electrical connections. Fortunately, modern technology provides practical solutions that are both simple to install and fairly inexpensive.

Whimsical fish or other decorative designs can serve attractively as companions to in-pool fountains.

Search for a self-contained fountain kit that includes a pump, plumbing, and electrical connections. Choose from fountains that bubble the water into an artistic basin and fountains that spray water in various patterns depending on the nozzle that is used. Fountain spray nozzles create a variety of patterns, including a simple spray, bell jet, two- or three-tier spray, whirling spray, or geyser. Some fountains drizzle water over a ledge, giving the impression of a waterfall. Others project the water from a small statue—dolphin, frog, duck, or swan. Make certain that fountain statuary is ceramic, cast-concrete, or plastic rather than lead, which can contaminate the water and cause problems for plants or animals.

A fountain in your garden adds movement and sound to an otherwise quiet setting. In addition to adding a special appeal to the water garden, a fountain offers other benefits. As the water is sprayed or bubbled through a fountain, it is aerated. This benefits fish and other aquatic life. If you include a filter as part of the setup, the water stays clearer.

▶ **Why stop with one fountain when you can have a grouping such as this wonderful heron with spouting fish that it hopes to catch?**

Art and Sculpture

A fountain may be an integral part of a sculpture or another object that offers an artistic appearance. You may find an appropriate sculpture or a sculptural object in an antique store. A large millstone, for instance, makes an attractive fountain. Smaller ones can serve handsomely as stepping stones.

A classical sculpture of a human figure adds elegance to a water garden. Place it at the edge of a pool where it and its reflection make a lovely focal point. Incorporate the sculpture into surrounding plants to make the artwork look right at home.

▲ Artistic cranes, ancient symbols of good luck in the Orient, make handsome garden sculptures and serve well as fountains.

Modern and abstract sculptures also serve a water garden well, providing intriguing shapes and patterns. Place an abstract sculpture directly in the garden or on an appropriate base. Placing a sculpture on a base often makes trimming and weeding easier than if you have to work around the sculpture itself. It also sets the art slightly above the surrounding ground level making it easier to appreciate the entire piece.

◀ A contorted piece of artfully arranged driftwood serves as sculpture bridging this water garden.

▼ Well-placed mirrors in the water garden can double the effect of the garden as well as increase its apparent depth.

Artists are not the only producers of garden sculpture. Nature also makes objects that have artistic qualities. You may choose to decorate your garden with "found art." Large pieces of driftwood, boulders, large tree branches, or whatever else you find may capture your interest because of their innate beauty.

Whenever you choose to feature a sculpture in your water garden, take advantage of the reflective quality of the water. Reflections become a part of the artwork as they change according to the light and the movement of the air.

A simple mirror can work as an artistic feature. Find a paned window frame or wooden storm door glass insert. Take it to a glass store and fit it with mirrored glass. Hang the frame on a wall near the water garden. The mirrored illusion doubles the size of the garden. Look into the mirror and it seems that you are looking into another garden.

CHAPTER HIGHLIGHTS

This chapter explains balanced water ecosystems, describes the cycles of the seasons, suggests regular maintenance routines, and tells you how to clean and repair water features.

MAINTAINING WATER GARDENS

As the seasons roll by, routine maintenance chores will keep your water garden and its accessories in tiptop shape. For the most part, the chores involve only light work that can be quite enjoyable. Care for a water feature by maintaining a natural order of events. The right pH and the right proportion of plants and fish to water are crucial in establishing an ecological balance in your garden pool.

Observation is the most important facet of maintenance. Notice indications that something should be done. As you spend leisure time around your water feature, learn what indicates an impending problem. This may be as simple as dead leaves on the water surface or a fountain that has lost some of its power. Address problems early on to avoid serious consequences for your garden pool and more work for you.

Become familiar with seasonal maintenance chores. From spring cleanup to summer care and fall preparation for winter, certain tasks will be repeated annually. Take care of them on a timely basis to save yourself the hassle and effort of repairing equipment and materials that have been poorly maintained.

A Balanced Ecosystem

The ecosystem of a water feature depends upon the water, the plants and animals, the amount of sunlight, the temperature, gases, and minerals. The size and shape of the pool, its surface area, and pH of the water also are factors that contribute to the health and balance of the system. When this created ecosystem is in balance, the water will be clear and the plants and animals will be healthy.

▼ A well-balanced pool will be clear and clean. Fish and plants will be displayed in full glory.

The ideal pH for fish is slightly alkaline, (7.0–8.0), although they usually do well if the pH ranges between 7.0 and 10.0. Use a pH meter or testing kit to check the pH every four to five weeks during warm weather. Algae raise the water pH by using carbon dioxide and removing carbonic acid from the water. Good filtration encourages a consistent pH. For the sake of fish and plant health, correct any pH deficiency gradually. Avoid changing the pH by

▲ Sometimes the water in a garden pool will get murky and green. This is often due to algae buildup. Block sunlight from reaching the water by covering more of the pond surface with floating plants or provide more aeration. In some cases an algicide may be necessary to remove the green coloration.

more than one unit at a time to minimize stress to the fish and plants.

In spring when first filling a pool, or after adding plants, algae bloom may turn the water green and murky, especially if the water is rich in nutrients. It's not necessary to empty the pool and start over. This is a stage that many pools go through. Be patient. Wait for the bloom to die back. Submerged and floating aquatic plants help control algae growth. Submerged plants compete for nutrients with the algae. Floating plants shade the water, denying algae the sunlight they need in order to grow. Once the aquatic plants are growing actively, the algae bloom may disappear as fast as it developed.

Seasonal Maintenance

▲ The water garden wakes up in the springtime. Cut back dead foliage so that new growth can burst forth minus the detracting reminders of last year's shoots.

Each year, a garden pool goes through predictable seasonal changes. Routine care and maintenance will help keep your garden pool in good health. Know what the routines are, and note on your calendar when to do them. This will keep them simple and easy to do. If you have a healthy, well-balanced mix of aquatic life, regular maintenance will keep them vital.

In the spring, remove the water heater, and clean and store it. Check the pH of the water to make sure that it is within the required range– 7.0–8.0. Cut back plant debris that has lasted through the winter. Add new floating plants each spring to shade the water and discourage algae bloom. Make certain that submerged plants begin their spring growth. They compete for nutrients with the algae and provide another

reason for the algae bloom to fade. Tidy up the water feature, netting detritus from the bottom. Reinstall pumps and filters that were stored during the winter. Make sure all pumps and filters are clean. Repair water features and their accessories as soon as the weather warms. Begin monitoring for pests and diseases.

During summer months check the water pH level every month. Clean filters and pump strainers every week or so. Remove dying or decaying plant foliage. Thin and prune vigorous plants that threaten to take over the water garden. Keep half of the water surface covered with floating plants to prevent algae growth. Summer heat and winds evaporate water from your water feature—as much as an inch in depth every few days. Replenish the water before the level gets low. If you replace 20 percent or more of the water at any one time, fish health can suffer. To avoid injury to your fish, use a commercial chloramine remover according to product directions. Sometimes, letting a garden hose trickle into the water feature during the day will be enough to solve the evaporation problem. If deer eat your plants or raccoons or herons take your fish, consider getting a motion-activated water jet to frighten them away. A well-trained dog or animal repellents are other options to keep the pests away.

▼ In the winter, the water garden takes on more muted tones of whites, grays, and browns, bringing serenity to the scene.

▲ The water garden looks quite different as it cycles through the seasons. In fall, bright colors of autumn leaves create a stunning display to accompany the pond.

Autumn brings falling leaves. Remove leaves from your water feature before they begin to decompose. If fall leaves are a serious problem, spread netting over the water surface to catch the leaves before they sink to the bottom. Periodically empty the netting. Cut back the old foliage of marginal plants after frost turns them brown. Store any tender plants indoors. If you don't plan to heat the water to prevent freezing, remove the pump, filter, and fountain for cleaning, maintenance, and storage. Store them in a sealed plastic bag.

Winter months in colder climates bring freezing conditions. If you overwinter fish in your pond, keep the water from freezing over with a floating pool or livestock tank heater. Get out the water heater and set it up before the water freezes. Noxious gases from decaying plant material can build up under ice. Cease feeding fish during cold winter months.

◀ **Cut down on water garden maintenance by periodically trimming, fertilizing, and replanting if needed.**

◀ Plant some new and interesting marginal plants in the spring. Adjust edging that may have heaved out of place during winter freeze-thaw cycles.

▶ In the fall, when cold weather threatens and temperatures begin to dip, lift water lilies for storage indoors. You can store water lilies in a garbage bag in a location that does not freeze.

Cleaning

Avoid routinely draining a water feature. You only need to empty a pool when it needs repairs or major cleaning, or if you want to enlarge or drastically change the water feature. Small pools need tidying up more often than larger features. Late spring is a good time for cleaning out the bottom of a water feature. By then the water plants are growing. They will be in good shape for splitting and replanting.

Pool sweeps or pond vacuums siphon water out of the system and make it much easier to perform cleanup chores. A siphon is powered by water flowing through a garden hose. A pond vacuum plugs into the pool's electrical supply and pumps water out of the pond. While you're cleaning the pool, net tadpoles, fish, or other aquatic life and put them in a holding container with fresh water that is no more than 18 inches deep and has been treated with chloramine remover. Another way to partially

You don't have to drain a garden pool often, but it is a major task when you do. Use a submersible pump to accomplish the job.

drain the pool is to use the pool's circulating pump. Attach a hose to the delivery outlet of the pump. Empty all of the water so that you can remove collected sludge from the bottom. Be careful when removing sediment from the pond bottom to avoid harm to the liner. After sludge removal is completed, refill the pond with water. Add any chemicals needed to remove chloramine and condition the water.

Clean the filter and intake screen of the pump at least every month, better yet, once a week. Occasionally, leaves or other debris clogs the intake of a pump. If this happens, disconnect the pump, remove the screen covering the intake, and then direct a hard stream of water from the garden hose to unclog the screen and the impeller. While you're at it, remove algae that may have built up.

Submersible pumps are sealed and self-lubricating. Avoid operating a submersible pump out of the water. Doing so may cause the motor to burn out.

As part of spring cleanup remove all the gunk and dead plants from the bottom and sides of the pool.

Scrub rocks and spillways to remove accumulated algae and other debris. A power washer makes short work of the task.

REPAIRS

▲ To clean a pump filter, unplug the device, lift it out of the pond, and use a strong blast from a garden hose to dislodge any particles or algae that may clog the filter.

It's usually easy to see when something goes wrong with a garden water feature. If there's a significant leak in a flexible liner, the water level drops faster than by evaporation alone. If a pump has a problem, its flow becomes slower and has less volume.

If something goes wrong with a fountain, its output is diminished. Diminished outflow from the fountain could be due to failure of either the pump or the fountainhead. Regularly clean pump filters to reduce fountain problems. Similarly, examine, unclog, and clean fountainheads and nozzles to eliminate that potential problem.

If the water level in a rigid fiberglass pool drops, check for probable causes. If the pool is not level, water may be spilling over the low edge. A stone or other sharp object pressing on the bottom of the pool may have cracked it. If someone stepped into the pool, it may have cracked. Whatever the cause, fiberglass is quite easy to repair. Fiberglass repair kits are available at automotive or water garden supply stores. Follow repair kit directions carefully. Since it's best to apply the fiberglass repair material to the bottom of the pool, take it completely out of the ground and turn it over to apply the repair.

The most difficult part of repairing a puncture or tear in a flexible EPDM liner is finding the leak. Sometimes you can discover the level of the leak by noting where the water level stops dropping—the leak will be at that level. Once you discover the source of the leak, scrub it clean and dry it completely. Repair kits that include double-sided adhesive tape are available at water garden supply stores. Wipe the damaged area with a soft cloth dampened with alcohol. Place the double-sided adhesive over the hole and press firmly. Wait a couple of minutes, until the adhesive becomes tacky, then press a patch of liner material firmly over the adhesive. Wait 12 hours before refilling the liner.

◀ Whether you have found the leak in a rigid liner, as shown, or in a flexible one, the repair process is similar. Begin by cleaning and drying the liner around the leak.

◀ Use a patch kit made for the type of liner and follow the instructions for applying the adhesive patch.

CHAPTER HIGHLIGHTS

This chapter describes plants and animals
you may wish to have in your water
garden, and how to care for them.

PLANTS AND ANIMALS FOR WATER GARDENS

Once you have completed the construction of your water feature, choose plants and animals to make the picture complete. Flowering and foliage plants thrive on, in, and next to the water. Choose water garden plants that blend well with the shrubs, perennials, and annuals in the rest of your garden.

Animals in the garden include both those you choose and, often, those that choose you. Koi and goldfish are decorative additions to a garden pool. In addition to looking lovely as they swim around, you can train them to come when you clap your hands or when you feed them. Beware of keeping koi in the same water feature with prized plants, as they are enthusiastic salad lovers. However, if you start with small koi and don't feed them, you can have your koi and prized plants, too. Snails help keep down algae. Turtles, frogs, toads, and salamanders may find their way into your garden waters.

PLANTS

Parrot's feather consumes excess nutrients from the water. Its foliage rises above the water's surface.

Water garden plants are grouped according to the role they play in water gardens. There are marginals, floaters, and submerged plants. The latter often are called oxygenators because their primary role is to add oxygen to the water, an asset for ecologically balanced pools.

Bog and marginal plants thrive poolside and in bogs or rain gardens. Water lilies, lotuses, and floating plants fill an important niche in the water garden. They have both flowers and handsome foliage.

Some water plants are hardy even in extremely cold climates, and others are tender. Take the tender ones indoors for the winter or replace them each spring. Some plants spread rampantly while others remain tidily within chosen confines. Each of these water plants has unique charm, aesthetic value, and environmental requirements.

◄ Plants whose leaves float on the surface occupy an important place in the water garden biota. Here, water clover and water lilies cover the pond surface.

▼ Marginal water garden plants such as these irises grow in shallow water at the edge of the water feature.

MOIST AREAS

Plants that thrive in wet soil or shallow water are the right choices for bog gardens. They also make good choices for rain gardens if you don't mind adding water during drought periods. Grow them in heavy soil. The soil pH should hover around 7.0, although most will tolerate soil that is slightly acidic or slightly alkaline.

These plants provide valuable accents of color, form, and texture as they visually soften the edges of a water feature. Marginal plants such as sweet flag, reed, rush, and cattail provide a sensuous rustle as the summer breezes swirl through the garden. For those that prove to be invasive, grow in containers.

▲ Plants for moist areas, for the edges of pools, for bog gardens, or for rain gardens, come in a variety of species that will thrive in these specialized areas.

If you grow marginal plants in containers along the edges of a pond, place the pots on bricks to raise them so that they rest in no more than 3 inches of water. Most of these plants also are considered marginal plants even though they may be happiest in the middle of a boggy situation. Flowering marginal plants include yellow flag iris, Siberian iris, swamp milkweed, flowering rush, pickerel weed, marsh marigold, and water canna.

FLOWERING RUSH

(Butomus umbellatus). This genus has only one species of aquatic perennial. It is also known as water gladiolus and is native to North America, Europe, and Asia. This plant grows in the same environment as cattails, in marshy places and shallow water at the edges of ponds. It grows up to 3 feet in height and has fragrant rose-color flowers that appear in late summer and are carried well above the surface of the water. The attractive dark green foliage is long, thin, and twisted. Zones 5–11.

DWARF WATER BAMBOO

(Dulichium arundinaceum). This is not a true bamboo, though its general appearance is similar. The plant is in the sedge family, although it's not a sedge either, because the hollows of its stems are round rather than triangular as in true sedges. The plant has short grasslike leaves at nearly every node. The small brownish flowers appear in summer. This moisture-loving plant grows in sun or shade. It grows up to 3 feet in height. Zones 4–11.

SPIKE RUSH

(Eleocharis obtusa). This genus of plants, which is in the same family as sedges, includes many semiaquatic and aquatic plants native from arctic to tropical regions throughout much of the world. The leaves are bladeless sheaths that look like spikes, thus the name. There are many of these strange spiky leaves. Summer flowers look like small brownish clubs at the ends of long stems. It thrives in partial shade as well as sun. Spike rush grows about 12 inches in height with equal width. Zones 3–11.

HORSETAIL

(Equisetum spp.). This genus includes about two dozen species native mostly to the Northern Hemisphere. Because of its rough texture, it is also called scouring rush. Native Americans and early Americans used the stems to scrub pots and dishes. Plant stems are green, jointed, and fluted. The leaves are whorls of minute, brownish scales that join to form sheaths. Plants do not bear true flowers. They spread by rhizomatous roots and can be invasive if not kept under control. Zones 4–11.

YELLOW FLAG

(Iris pseudacorus). Also called yellow water iris, this native of Europe to western Asia is a vigorous sun-loving plant. It has flat, swordlike, ribbed leaves that are grayish green. The plant grows up to 36 inches in height. It bears spring flowers with petals that are yellow with darker markings and falls that have darker yellow zones. Each branched flower stem will bear at least four, and sometimes as many as a dozen, flowers. There are variegated cultivars of this species. Zones 4–9.

SIBERIAN IRIS

(Iris sibirica). This species, native to eastern Europe and western Asia, is at its best in full sun with soil that is moist to wet. Leaves are thin and swordlike. The foliage looks almost like grass. Flowers are elegant iris forms. There are many beautiful varieties of Siberian irises with flowers of white to blue to lavender. One of the most popular is an early-blooming cultivar, 'Caesar's Brother', with dark purple flowers. The plants will grow 24 to 36 inches in height. Zones 4–9.

WATER ARUM

(Peltandra virginica). This North American native arum, cousin to Jack-in-the-pulpit, is found in bogs, swamps, and ditches, mostly in the eastern half of the United States. The leaves are shaped like arrowheads and each have three prominent veins, one median and two into the lobes. Hooded flowers have narrow greenish spathes that surround the fleshy clublike spadix. The fruits are red. Water arum will thrive in full sun to partial shade. It grows up to 18 inches in height. Zones 5–9.

PICKEREL WEED

(Pontederia cordata). This native of marshy areas of the Americas has glossy heart-shape leaves on long stems. The leaves may be floating or submerged. Tubular bluish-purple flowers appear from late spring into fall. There also are varieties with white flowers or with deep mauve-blue flowers. Clumps of pickerel weed or pickerel rush can grow as tall as 30 inches with a spread of 18 inches. Grow this plant in full sun. The ripe fruits of pickerel rush are edible either raw or dried, and the young leaves are tasty in salads or when steamed. Zones 5–11.

BROADLEAF ARROWHEAD

(Sagittaria latifolia). This aquatic native of North America grows from large tubers that ducks as well as people may use as food. The leaves are mainly shaped like arrows and grow above the water surface. Clusters of whorled white flowers appear on 4-foot stems during summer months. Where conditions are good, this plant may grow up to 3 feet in height with a spread of 3 feet. Arrowheads will grow in full sun to partial shade. There are several varieties with unusual foliage or flowers. Zones 5–11.

LIZARD'S TAIL

(Saururus cernuus). Lizard's tail, also called swamp lily or water dragon, is native to eastern North America. It has heart-shape bright green leaves. The waxy flowers are whitish or ivory and fragrant. They grow on curvy spikes that do indeed resemble a lizard's tail. The spreading rhizomes form plant clumps that grow 12–24 inches in height. Lizard's tail will grow in full sun to partial shade. Zones 5–11.

NARROW-LEAVED CATTAIL

(Typha angustifolia). Also called graceful cattail or lesser bullrush, this plant is native to the Americas, Europe, northern Africa, and Asia. This species has slender leaves that sway gracefully in the slightest breath of air. The typical bullrush flowers consist of cylinders of dark brown female flowers topped by a spike of lighter brown male flowers. Narrow-leaved cattail will thrive in sun to partial shade. It grows 3–4 feet in height. Zones 3–11.

BROADLEAF CATTAIL

(Typha latifolia). Broadleaf cattail or bullrush is native to parts of North America, Europe, Asia, and northern Africa. This is the cattail we commonly see growing in wetlands and marshy places. This plant thrives in sun to partial shade. There is a handsome variegated form. Cattails provide strong vertical lines to a water garden, a great asset in garden design. Cattail roots and young shoots are edible. The plant grows up to 7 feet in height. Zones 3–11.

MARGINALS

Marginal plants are mostly perennial and often decorative. You will find them in the shallow water of ponds and pools as well as in slow-moving streams. They grow well in moist areas where the water is 4–12 inches deep. Marginal plants have their roots in soil, and foliage that either is upright or floats on shallow water whereas the moisture-loving plants will grow well in slightly drier conditions. True marginals should have wet soil around their roots at all times.

Many marginal plants have to be gradually acclimatized to water that is 4–12 inches deep over the soil surface as it may be near the edges of water features or natural ponds. Some will thrive with water around their roots at varying depths while others need to be kept in water only an inch or so deep for the first few months—then they can be in a slightly deeper site. A number of marginal plants are more or less invasive and therefore might better serve water garden needs if grown in containers and often lifted for dividing or root pruning.

▼ **Marginal plants play an important design role as they fill the space between the pond bank and the open water.**

JAPANESE SWEET FLAG

(Acorus gramineus). This semievergreen is native to eastern Asia. The foliage grows in fans of grasslike leaves that are fine and tapering, up to 14 inches in length. The rich green leaves are bright and glossy. There are several fine cultivars of this plant with special characteristics including variegated foliage, small size, and compactness. As the flowers are inconspicuous, these plants are grown for their graceful foliage that offers good vertical lines to the water garden. The plants will form clumps up to 12 inches tall and wide. Zones 4–11.

WATER PLAINTAIN

(Alisma plantago-aquatica). Water plantain is a deciduous rhizomatous plant. This marginal aquatic, native to temperate regions of North America, Europe, eastern Asia, and Africa, grows in large colonies at the edge of ponds or pools. Basal rosettes of gray green, plantainlike leaves grow on long stems. The leaves are oval to lanceolate with pointed tips. Clusters of small, whitish to pinkish-white flowers appear in mid- to late summer. The three-petal flowers are shaped like saucers. Water plantain grows best in full sun, reaching up to 30 inches in height. Zones 5–8.

UMBRELLA PALM

(Cyperus alternifolius). This sedge is evergreen and is native to wet tropical areas of Africa. The typical sedge stems are sturdy, leafless, and triangular in cross section. Beautiful compound umbels of flowers develop during the summer. Two varieties offer worthwhile characteristics: 'Miniature' is smaller than the species, and 'Zebra' has yellow stripes on the stems. Both the species and the cultivars are sensational plants for water's edge in ponds and pools. Umbrella palm will grow well in full sun to partial shade. It may reach more than 3 feet in height. Zones 9–11.

CHINESE WATER CHESTNUT

(Eleocharis dulcis). This Asian native is in the same family as papyrus and is a tuberous perennial of warm regions. The water chestnuts are edible and common in Oriental stir-fried dishes. The plants are bright green and grow in thick clumps. The small leaves are simple reddish-brown, pointed sheaths on the stems. Spiky brown flowers appear in summer. Water chestnut thrives in full sun to partial shade. You can grow Chinese water chestnut indoors as a houseplant during winter months. The plant grows up to 12 inches in height with equal width. Zones 8–11.

VARIEGATED MANNA GRASS

(Glyceria maxima 'Variegata'). This true grass, native to temperate regions of Eurasia, grows vigorously and spreads well, which may be a good reason to keep it in a container at the edge of a garden pool. The leaves, with a pinkish tinge on the new growth, are narrow and have keels. Leaves grow up to 24 inches in length. Vertical stripes of green, white, and creamy white make the foliage stunning. Brown flowerheads, often with a purplish tint, appear in summer. Variegated manna grass grows up to 32 inches in height. Zones 5–11.

WATER PURSLANE

(Ludwigia palustris). This native of the Americas, Europe, and Asia is a mat-forming plant that will grow floating in water or under the surface where it gives the effect of an underwater groundcover. Weak stems bear lance-shape to oval leaves that are pointed and 2 inches or less in length. Leaves are bright glossy green or purple above and dark olive to purple underneath. Strands of this plant grow up to 20 inches long. Tiny yellow flowers that appear in summer are inconspicuous. Water purslane grows best in full sun although it tolerates some shade. Zones 5–11.

FOUR-LEAF WATER CLOVER

(Marsilea mutica). This Australian native is a true fern although its fronds look more like four-leaf clover or oxalis. This creeping aquatic plant develops stems up to 24 inches long. Thin threadlike stems support light green leaves that float on the water surface. The pale green leaves have four leaflets that are somewhat triangular with rounded outer edges. Each leaflet has two zones of green. A tan or light green band is between the two green zones. It grows well in full sun to partial shade. Zones 9–11.

WATERMINT

(Mentha aquatica). This Eurasian native is a true mint and one of those that can spread quickly. Grow it in a container to limit its spread. The plant has long, thin rhizomes that are segmented. Stems are often tinged with a reddish-purple color and aromatic leaves are equal and opposite like other mints. Leaves are dark green and hairy. Dense flowerheads of lavender flowers appear in summer. Flowers are fragrant and attract butterflies. Watermint grows up to 12 inches in height and has a spreading growth habit. Zones 5–11.

WATER SNOWFLAKE

(Nymphoides cristata). This Australian native is rhizomatous and grows in shallow water where it spreads rapidly. It will grow in as little as 4 inches of water. The mat of plants soon looks like a floating green carpet. The 2- to 3-inch yellowish-green leaves are oval and have brownish-red markings. The small ½-inch white flowers appear in spring and continue blooming into late fall. The flowers have yellow stamens, look like stars, and are fragrant. Water snowflake grows up to 24 inches tall. Zones 7–11.

GOLDEN CLUB

(Orontium aquaticum). This native of eastern North America is an aquatic aroid. Golden club looks great as part of an informal waterside planting. It has narrow elliptical leaves that may be under or above the water level. The leaves are hairy, velvety, and dark green. The spathes (sheathing bracts) that first appear in the flowers soon wilt, leaving cylindrical spadices that are yellow above whitish stalks. Golden club grows from thick rhizomes in partial sun to shade. It grows up to 10 inches in height with a spread of up to 16 inches. Zones 6–11.

GREATER SPEARWORT

(Ranunculus lingua). This marginal aquatic, native from
Europe to Siberia, has hollow erect stems with oblong
narrow, bluish-green 8-inch-long leaves with cordate
bases. The buttercup-yellow flowers appear in early
summer. Flowers are up to 2 inches in diameter and are
cup shape. Not fussy, greater spearwort will grow in sun
or shade. The plant grows up to 36 inches in height and
spreads by stoloniferous roots. Containerize this plant to
control its spread. Zones 4–9.

PURPLE THALIA

(Thalia dealbata). Purple thalia, or hardy canna, is native
to Mexico and the southern United States. It grows in the
marshy edges of lakes and ponds. The handsome long-
stem leaves are powdery gray green with a bluish cast.
The leaves grow up to 20 inches in length, making a
strong statement in the landscape. Purple summer flowers
grow in slender clusters that are up to 8 inches long. This
plant may reach a height of 6 feet, yet may only have a
spread of about 2 feet. Zones 7–11.

WATER LILIES

Water lilies thrive when growing in still water in full sun. Water lilies are vigorous when planted in garden soil with aquatic fertilizer. Experts recommend fertilizing several times each season. Use aquatic fertilizer tablets made for this purpose. Use containers made for growing water lilies.

Plant hardy water lilies outdoors when the water temperature reaches 60°F. Fill the container about ⅔ full with commercial water garden potting soil. Plant tubers in center, spreading out the roots. Fill over roots. Hardy varieties can spend the winter in the garden pond as long as the roots don't freeze. Necessary water depth will depend on the zone of your garden.

Plant tropical water lilies when water temperature reaches 65°F. Fill containers to about ⅔ full with a heavy clay soil. Plant tubers in center, spreading out the roots. Fill soil over the roots. When the water cools in the fall, take tropicals indoors or into a greenhouse to store until spring.

With all water lilies, cover the top of the soil with pea gravel or coarse sand so that soil does not cloud the water. When purchasing water lilies, check to see what they are and what their requirements are: tropical or hardy, day-blooming or night-blooming, flower color, required water depth, and eventual spread on the water surface.

▲ **Water lilies are favorites of water gardeners all around the world. They come in a wide variety of sizes and types. This one is 'Colorado'.**

HARDY WATER LILIES

EUROPEAN WHITE WATER LILY

(Nymphaea alba). This native of Eurasia and northern Africa bears slightly fragrant summer flowers of pure white with stamens that are from yellow to orange. The large flowers, floating on the water surface, open in the morning and stay open until afternoon. Broadly oval, entire leaves up to 12 inches in diameter are dark green on top and usually reddish green underneath. This plant is part of the heritage of many hardy water lily cultivars. Zones 5–11.

FRAGRANT WATER LILY

(Nymphaea odorata). This native of the lakes and ponds of the eastern United States has fragrant white flowers up to 6 inches in diameter that appear from summer to fall. The flowers, usually floating on the water surface, open in early morning and stay open until afternoon. The 10-inch leaves are round and entire. They are dark green on top and purple with a rough texture underneath. Many fine hardy cultivars have been bred from this lovely water lily. Zones 3–11.

AURORA WATER LILY

(Nymphaea 'Aurora'). This hardy miniature water lily is one of several varieties in the red- to yellow-color changeable category. 'Aurora' flowers are 2–4 inches in diameter. When the flowers first open, they are creamy yellow to yellowish apricot. They darken as they mature. By the third day, they are dark red. This variety is a good choice for a small garden pool or large tub water garden. 'Aurora' will grow in water that is from under a foot to 2 feet in depth and may cover a 3-foot diameter. Zones 3–11.

CHROMATELLA WATER LILY

(Nymphaea 'Chromatella'). This hardy water lily with yellow flowers is floriferous with as little as three to five hours of direct sunlight per day. The flowers measure 2–6 inches in diameter, are cup shape, and creamy yellow. The leaves are mottled green. The mature spread ranges from 1–8 square feet, making this water lily a possibility for tub gardens. Blossoms stay open later in the afternoon than many of the other hardy water lilies. Zones 3–11.

PINK SENSATION WATER LILY

(Nymphaea 'Pink Sensation'). This is one of the longtime favorites of the pink hardy water lilies. It is extremely floriferous and the flowers stay open until late afternoon. The 6-inch flowers are clear rich pink with white edges. Flowers open cup shape, gradually becoming star shape. Outer stamens are pink and inner ones are yellow. The leaves are purplish when they first emerge and round with narrow sinuses. The mature plant has a spread of 3–6 feet. Zones 3–11.

PYGMY WATER LILY

(Nymphaea tetragona). This naturally small species is native from northeastern Europe to northern Asia and North America. The small 1- to 2-inch floating flowers are creamy white, pink, or red, and slightly fragrant. The 4-inch oval leaves are green with brown spots. The undersides of the leaves are reddish-green. Its small size recommends it for small water gardens. The pygmy water lily comes in a number of attractive cultivars including 'Alba' with white flowers, rosy pink 'Joanne Pring' *(above)*, and deep red 'Rubis'. Zones 3–11.

DAY-BLOOMING TROPICAL WATER LILIES

CAPE BLUE WATER LILY

(Nymphaea capensis). This tropical day-blooming water lily is also known as blue capensis. It is native to Africa, and has pale blue flowers that are star shape and fragrant. The stamens are yellow and the flower is a sensational 8–10 inches in diameter. The round 10- to 16-inch leaves have toothed undulating edges and lobes that overlap. The leaves are medium green. This species is in the heritage of many modern varieties. Zones 10–11.

AUSTRALIAN WATER LILY

(Nymphaea gigantea). Also known as 'Blue Gigantea' this tropical native of Papua, New Guinea and Australia has flowers up to 12 inches in diameter. The color is blue to purplish blue with bright yellow stamens. The medium-green, oval leaves are up to 24 inches in diameter with finely toothed, wavy edges. The bottoms of the leaves are tinged purple to pink. The lobes may overlap. It must have water that is 80°F or more to thrive and bloom. Zones 10–11.

DAY-BLOOMING TROPICAL WATER LILIES (CONTINUED)

MRS. GEORGE H. PRING WATER LILY

(*Nymphaea* 'Mrs. George H. Pring'). This is one of many tropical water lilies that the late George H. Pring bred during his long, productive career at the Missouri Botanical Garden. This variety, bred in 1932, is a day-blooming tropical water lily with handsome off-white flowers. The flowers are fragrant and grow up to 8 inches in diameter. Leaves are green with red mottling. This prolific bloomer covers an area of up to 12 square feet, and thus is suitable only for medium to large garden pools. The cultivar 'Alice Tricker', created in 1937, is an improved form of 'Mrs. George H. Pring'. Zones 10–11.

NIGHT-BLOOMING TROPICAL WATER LILIES

MISSOURI WATER LILY

(Nymphaea 'Missouri'). In 1932, George Pring created this night-blooming tropical water lily. It has creamy white flowers that are fragrant. The flowers may grow up to 12 inches in diameter. They have wide petals and a starlike appearance. Their eventual spread of 8 square feet or more limits them to medium to large garden pools. Young leaves of a metallic brown mature to green and have distinctive fluted edges that allow water to partially cover the lily pads. Zones 10–11.

MRS. GEORGE C. HITCHCOCK WATER LILY

(Nymphaea 'Mrs. George C. Hitchcock'). This variety, dating from 1926, is another of George Pring's creations. It is floriferous and continues blooming late in the season. The pink flowers with outer petals of darker pink grow up to 12 inches in diameter. They show up beautifully at night. A bonus is its fragrance. Since this water lily spreads up to 12 square feet, it is a plant only for a medium to large garden pool. Zones 10–11.

RED FLARE WATER LILY

(Nymphaea 'Red Flare'). This night-blooming tropical water lily has deep, vivid mahogany-red flowers up to 10 inches in diameter. They are fragrant, a plus for the night garden. The long, narrow petals give this variety a starlike appearance. The stamens are pale pink to yellow. The foliage is maroon. The plant eventually covers up to 8 square feet, making it a good choice for medium to large pools. Zones 10–11.

LOTUSES

The two species of lotuses are in the genus *Nelumbo* and are native to eastern North America, Asia, and northern Australia. The lotus is a sacred symbol to Buddhists. Native Americans used native lotuses medicinally and for food. Oriental cooks favor the edible tubers of lotuses. Since they spread quite rapidly, grow them in large containers, using clay or sandy loam soil topped with a layer of pea gravel to keep the soil from clouding the water. They are heavy feeders, therefore use slow-release fertilizer or fertilize once or twice a month with water lily pelletized fertilizer. Lotuses require full sun. Protect the roots from freezing during the cold season. Either keep them in deep water or bring them inside or to a greenhouse. Store the rhizomatous roots in damp sand over the winter months or store the potted plant in a sealed plastic bag in a cool, dark place. Although most lotuses are hardy in Zones 6–11, they need several weeks of hot sunny weather to perform well. Flowers first appear in midsummer. The flowers are held just above the parasollike leaves that also rise above the water surface.

When buying lotuses, be sure to note their hardiness Zones, their eventual spread, and other specifics to the varieties you choose.

▼ **Lotuses, with their glorious blooms, impressive foliage, and saltshaker seedpods, are revered objects in the Orient. This is sacred lotus** *(Nelumbo nucifera)*.

AMERICAN LOTUS

(Nelumbo lutea). The American lotus or water chinquapin is native to eastern North America. The 10-inch flowers are double and creamy yellow with the typical lotus flower center that looks like a saltshaker and develops into decorative 4-inch seedpods often used in dried arrangements. Bluish-green rounded leaves are concave and grow up to 20 inches in diameter. The undersides of the leaves have prominent veining. The leaves rise directly from the rootstock on stems up to 6 feet tall. Zones 6–11.

ALBA GRANDIFLORA LOTUS

(Nelumbo 'Alba Grandiflora'). This lotus, descended from the sacred lotus, has leaves that are dark green with undulating edges. The single flowers are pure white and grow up to 10 inches in diameter. The flowers are fragrant with rounded petals. In this species, the leaves sometimes grow taller than the flowers, which results in flowers that are partially hidden. This plant grows up to 6 feet in height. Zones 8–11.

BABY DOLL LOTUS

(Nelumbo 'Baby Doll'). This is a lotus that grows to a height of 3–5 feet, somewhat shorter than the usual robust 6-footers. This lotus also has a comparatively small spread. Thus it can be grown in a tub on a patio or deck in as little as 6 inches of water. 'Baby Doll' is a gorgeous American hybrid featuring silky pure-white single flowers that grow up to 6 inches in diameter. Flat blue-green round leaves grow on short sturdy stems. Zones 7–11.

CHAWAN BASU LOTUS

(Nelumbo 'Chawan Basu'). This Asian-bred cultivar, another descendent of the sacred lotus, is floriferous. Its many flowers are pink with white centers. This semidwarf cultivar grows only to a height of about 3 feet with a fairly small spread. It is a good choice for smaller water gardens or for growing in containers. Zones 8–11.

MOMO BOTAN LOTUS

(Nelumbo 'Momo Botan'). This Asian-bred variety descends from the sacred lotus. It grows only to about 3 feet in height and develops a small to medium spread. This lotus is a good prospect for a small garden pool or for growing in a container. The double flowers are long-lasting and grow up to 6 inches in diameter. Each dark-pink petal lightens to yellow at its base. A related but even smaller cultivar is 'Momo Botan Minima' that grows only up to 18 inches in height and has smaller leaves. Zones 8–11.

MRS. PERRY D. SLOCUM LOTUS

(Nelumbo 'Mrs. Perry D. Slocum'). A free-flowering hybrid of the American lotus and the sacred lotus 'Rosea Plena', 'Mrs. Perry D. Slocum' has roundish gray-green leaves up to 30 inches or more in diameter with margins that may be flat or wavy. Growing to a height of 5 feet, this variety bears 12-inch summer flowers that emerge deep pink and gradually turn yellow over several days as they mature. The flowers are double and wonderfully fragrant. Zones 8–10.

PERRY'S SUPER STAR LOTUS

(Nelumbo 'Perry's Super Star'). This cultivar, a favorite of many, has blue-green leaves. The 6- to 8-inch flowers emerge rich pink. The pink gradually changes to yellow and then to creamy white with pink-tip petals. An unusual characteristic of the flowers is that there are up to eight petals near the centers that are tipped with green. The flowers are sweetly fragrant. These lotuses grow up to 4 feet in height. Zones 8–10.

ROSEA PLENA LOTUS

(Nelumbo 'Rosea Plena'). An Asian hybrid, this lotus bears huge double rose-pink flowers that have yellow centers. They are wonderfully fragrant and up to 12 inches in diameter. Oddly, although the flower is extremely large, the seedpod is quite small for a lotus. This variety is free-flowering. The leaves will grow up to 20 inches in diameter. It grows up to 5 feet in height and would be a good choice for medium to large pools. Zones 8–10.

SHIROKUNSHI LOTUS

(Nelumbo 'Shirokunshi'). This variety, a descendent of the sacred lotus, grows only up to 24 inches in height with a small spread. It is a good choice for medium-size ponds. It also would be suitable for growing in small pools, tubs, or large containers. The creamy white, 6- to 8-inch flowers are tulip shape and delightfully fragrant. Zones 8–10.

SACRED LOTUS

(Nelumbo nucifera). The sacred lotus is native to warm regions of Asia, the Middle East, and Australia. It has flat round leaves up to 32 inches in diameter. The leaves rise high above the water on stems up to 6 feet tall. The undersides of the leaves have prominent veining. Summer flowers, often double, are up to 12 inches in diameter. They emerge as a rose pink that gradually changes to paler pink as they age. Zones 8–11.

FLOATING PLANTS

Planting floating plants is simple. Place them on the water surface. Their roots hang down into the water. The smaller types that carpet the water surface will quickly establish themselves and thrive. The larger types may take a few days to settle in, but they also will soon appear as though they'd been there forever. The floaters help control algae by shading the water. If they are too successful, just scoop the excess plants from the water and put them on the compost pile. Some floating plants are native to temperate zones and can live through winter weather. Others, from warmer climates, will have to be taken indoors or into a greenhouse during cold weather. Some gardeners simply take a few of the tender plants indoors and grow them in a bowl of water or an aquarium during winter months. Others treat the tender floating plants as annuals, buying them new each spring. Some of these floating plants are rampant growers from warmer climates. Some can only be sold in areas that have killing frosts. Water hyacinth is a good example of a plant that is an invasive thug in warm climates but perfectly fine to plant in more northern climes. Many floating plants are great water purifiers. Plan to have about a third of the water surface covered by floating plants.

◀ Floating plants are easy to grow and can perform valuable service by controlling algae. Fairy moss and water lettuce cover the surface of this container water garden.

FAIRY MOSS

(Azolla spp.). Also known as mosquito fern and water fern, this floating plant makes a rich green carpet on the water surface. These small floating ferns survive cold months by means of small submerged plant fragments. Soft leaf clusters each have a tiny root. Fairy moss plants are richly green during warm weather. They turn pinkish purple when the weather turns cool. Since these are rampant spreaders, do not plant them in natural lakes or ponds. Zones 7–11.

WATER HYACINTH

(Eichhornia crassipes). This plant, native to tropical South America, and naturalized in too many places, is the king of rampant water plants in warm climates. Do not grow it south of the Mason-Dixon Line. But it's great in northern waters where it will die when hard frost hits it. Showy summer flowers are over an inch in diameter and funnel shape. They are pinkish lavender with yellow spots on the upper petals. Rosettes of green leaves with swollen bases grow to about 6 inches in diameter. Zones 10–11.

FROGBIT

(Hydrocharis morsus-ranae). Native in Eurasia and northern Africa, frogbit is a small plant cultivated for its dainty foliage and pretty three-petal white flowers. Not a true floating plant, its small leaves grow on short stems and are medium to dark green. Leaves are 2½ inches in diameter or less and round to kidney shape. Tiny floating sacs are on the undersides of the leaves. The plants may float or grow under the water. The foliage forms attractive mats. Plants grow side runners and may form roots that anchor in the silt or mud bottom. It will grow in partial shade to full sun, and overwinters by means of "buds" that sink to the bottom. Zones 4–11.

WATER POPPY

(Hydrocleys nymphoides). Native to South America, the water poppy may be free-floating or more commonly takes root in shallow water. The cup-shape yellow flower with its purple center has three petals and is 2–3 inches in diameter. The summer flowers appear just above the water surface when water temperature is 70°F or more. Long-stem floating leaves are broad, oval, and heart shape at their bases. Although the plant has stoloniferous shoots and may spread up to 6 feet, it is quite easy to control in cooler climates. Zones 10–11.

LESSER DUCKWEED

(Lemna minor). Duckweed, frog's buttons, or duckmeat, whatever you call it, this plant is native to many mild temperate climates and is hardy to Zone 4. The small leaves, just ⅛ inch wide, are round to nearly round. Flowers are tiny and inconspicuous. While it does form an attractive green floating mat, duckweed may be so successful that it becomes a nuisance. On the other hand, fish eat duckweed and may be all the control you need. Duckweed may appear in your water garden even if you don't plant it since it arrives on birds' feet. Scoop or net excess plants from the pool surface. Zones 4–11.

SENSITIVE PLANT

(Neptunia aquatica). Native to warm regions of South America, sensitive plant is a spreading plant with fuzzy yellow flowers 1 inch in diameter that appear throughout the summer. It is called sensitive because the leaves fold up when you touch it, like its cousin the mimosa. Both of these plants are legumes, members of the pea family. It grows in partial shade to full sun. Leaves are opposite and featherlike. The stems run along the water surface as the plant forms mats that become thicker throughout summer. This plant often will take root in shallow water. Zones 7–11.

FLOATING PLANTS (CONTINUED)

FLOATING HEART

(Nymphoides spp.). Several species of floating heart grow in temperate parts of the world, including at least two that are native to eastern North America, *N. aquatica* and *N. cordata.* A nice thing about the floating hearts is that they tolerate moving water. This feature makes them useful alternatives to water lilies. These plants spread rapidly, their round to kidney-shape leaves forming green carpets. They root into soil in shallow water. The fringed yellow or white flowers grow above the water surface. Zones 5–10.

WATER LETTUCE

(Pistia stratoites). Also known as shell flower, this African native is a cousin of Jack-in-the-pulpit. It has become an invasive plant in lakes and rivers of tropical and subtropical regions. Yet it is an attractive ornamental for temperate water gardens. Feathery roots hang below pale green rosettes of wedge-shape, fluted leaves that each may be up to a foot long and several inches wide. Flowers are inconspicuous. Water lettuce spreads by offsets that appear at the base of the plant. Plants may reach up to 24 inches in diameter. Zones 10–11.

WILLOW GRASS

(Polygonum amphibium). Native to warm temperate regions, this plant has leaves up to 4 inches long. They are oblong to lanceolate with 1-inch petioles. Like other polygonums, the leaves have prominent midribs and may have a reddish color. Leaves float on the surface of the water. Pink to red summer flowers grow in tight spikes above the water surface. Willow grass grows in partial shade to full sun in marshy areas. It is not a true floating plant because it roots into soil. Zones 5–11.

VELVET LEAF

(Salvinia molesta). This free-floating rootless plant, also known as butterfly fern, is native to tropical regions of Central and South America. This tender perennial fern has become rampant in warm areas where it is a noxious weed. Yet it is an attractive plant for garden pools in cold temperate regions. The hairy leaves of this species are pale green, round or oval, and grow thickly on thin stems. Leaves are about an inch wide. Velvet leaf grows in partial shade. Koi find it tasty. Zones 10–11.

SUBMERGED PLANTS

Submerged plants used to be known as oxygenators because they add oxygen to the water during daylight hours. At night they absorb carbon dioxide for structural growth. These are nature's own natural water purifiers, removing excess and unwanted nutrients from the water. This helps prevent algae buildup. Algae thrive in nutrient-rich water that is in full sun. These plants grow completely under the water surface and have weak stems that will not support them. They may have flower stalks that rise above the water surface. Plants in this group vary greatly and not all will thrive in your garden pool, so grow several varieties to see what does best. These tend to spread rapidly and so should be regularly thinned. Submerbed plants generally are sold in bunches that have rubber bands around the stems. A good rule of thumb is to have one bunch for every square foot of water surface. You can push the stems into heavy soil or gravel, or just let them be free in the water.

◀ Parrot's feather (*Myriophyllum aquaticum)* acts as a good water purifier because it uses up excess nutrients from the water.

FANWORT

(Cabomba caroliniana). Fanwort is a submerged plant native
to central and southeastern United States. It has oblong
leaves that are bright green and grow 2–3 inches in length.
Summer flowers are small and white with yellow centers.
Whorls of delicate leaves make good hiding places for fish.
They also are a favorite food of fish, especially during the
cold season. Fanwort thrives in full sun to partial shade
where water is cool. A single plant may spread about
12 inches wide. Zones 5–11.

STARWORT

(Callitriche spp.). This genus includes a couple of dozen
mostly aquatic perennials from marshy sites in Europe,
Asia, and North America. Leaves may form rosettes that
look like stars. The submerged leaves appear translucent
and form a tangled mat. Summer flowers are small,
solitary, and white. Underwater foliage is sparse while
that near the surface is thicker. The leaves grow into bright
green mats that are extremely dense. Fish enjoy grazing
on starwort. Zones 3–8.

SUBMERGED PLANTS (CONTINUED)

HORNWORT

(Ceratophyllum demersum). This native of Mediterranean Europe and tropical Africa is a bushy, many-branched plant that is generally rootless and floats freely. Dark-green leaves grow in whorls. The slender stems grow up to 24 inches in length. Tiny white flowers are insignificant. Hornwort tolerates a wide range of water conditions. The plant's assets are its delicate foliage and its success at outcompeting algae. It sinks to the bottom during winter months. Zones 6–9.

WATER THYME

(Egeria densa). Native to South America, this submerged plant has naturalized in many other regions with warm climates. The many-branched stems, up to 3 feet in length with a spread of about 12 inches, have linear pointed leaves that are stemless and grow in whorls. The leaves are shiny and bright green. Small white, three-petal flowers appear in summer and are carried above the water surface. A noxious weed in warm areas, grow this one only where it will not survive cold winters. Zones 9–11.

CANADIAN PONDWEED

(Elodea canadensis). Canadian pondweed or ditchweed is native to North America and has naturalized widely throughout much of Europe. The dark-green translucent foliage grows on brittle branching stems that may reach 5 feet or more in length. Lanceolate to oval leaves are finely toothed. Late summer flowers are tiny and grow in leaf axils. Canadian pondweed grows in full sun to partial shade. Many fish like to eat pondweed. The plant can become a serious pest if it escapes into streams or natural waterways. Zones 4–11.

WILLOW MOSS

(Fontinalis antipyretica). Also known as water moss, this native of North America, Eurasia, and northern Africa is a dark olive-green plant with branching stems that are covered by scalelike leaves. This is a great plant for sheltering spawning fish and their fry—fish eggs stick to the leaves. While there are a number of species that might serve as well, this is the most available one. This slow-growing plant prefers water that is clear and slowly moving, and partial shade. Zones 5–11.

WATER VIOLET

(Hottonia palustris). This member of the primrose family, native to Europe and western Asia, has delicate light-green foliage with finely cut leaves. Masses of leaves grow both above and below the water surface. Pinnate leaves are stemless and light green. Spikes of pale pinkish-lilac flowers with yellow centers rise above the water in the spring. The flowers are five-petal and resemble primroses. Zones 5–9.

PARROT'S FEATHER

(Myriophyllum spp.). This genus includes a number of aquatic plants found in many parts of the world. The plants have fine feathery foliage that may be green, olive-green, or brownish green. The decorative foliage may grow totally submerged or partially emergent. Some species have small spikes of early summer flowers that grow an inch or so above the water surface. Zones 3–10.

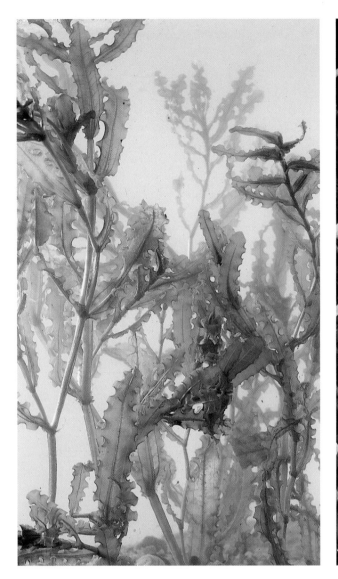

CURLED PONDWEED

(Potamogeton crispus). This European native now grows wild in California and the eastern United States. Curled pondweed has creeping rhizomes that branch and spread over pond bottoms. The rhizomes give rise to translucent lanceolate underwater foliage and tough opaque floating leaves. Leaves are reddish green, curly, oblong, and narrow, about 1½ inches in length. Stems are up to 6 feet long. White flowers are carried just above the water surface in summer. Curled pondweed may be invasive in natural water features with earthen bottoms. Zones 7–11.

YELLOW WATER BUTTERCUP

(Ranunculus flabellaris). This North American native grows submerged or floating. It bears yellow flowers in spring and summer. The 1-inch flowers resemble buttercups. The plants have finely cut leaves and stiff stems. They form large colonies that are quite lovely, especially when in flower. Water crowfoot does not become invasive, making it a good choice for water garden pools and ponds. It grows best in full sun. Zones 4–11.

UNDERWATER ARROWHEAD

(Sagittaria natans). A United States native, underwater arrowhead has green strappy translucent leaves up to 6 inches long that rise from the base, giving the plant a grasslike appearance. Tuck the roots of this plant into a container or into gravel on the bottom of the pool. In shallow water it produces a single white flower slightly under an inch in diameter. One of the earliest underwater plants to begin growing in the spring, it competes well with algae for excess nutrients, providing good algae control. It grows in partial shade to full sun. Zones 6–11.

EELGRASS

(Vallisneria spiralis). Eelgrass, ribbon grass, or tape grass is native to Eurasia, Africa, and Australia. It has tightly spiraled, ribbonlike, translucent pale-green leaves. Leaves will grow up to 32 inches in length. The rippling leaves can be very attractive, especially in moving water. Greenish female flowers float at the water surface. They appear throughout the growing season. Male flowers appear underwater, then float to the surface. Eelgrass grows well in partial shade to sunny locations. Zones 8–11.

ANIMALS

▲ Common goldfish are beautiful in a garden pool, providing motion and interest.

◀ Most elegant of the pond fish are koi, the ornamental fish that have long been favorites in Oriental gardens.

Animals of many kinds can play parts in the life of your water garden features. There are those that you introduce on purpose and those that just appear. The combination of land and water plus sheltering plants will attract local wildlife to your water garden.

Most commonly, gardeners introduce fish into their water gardens. The carp we know as goldfish and koi are colorful additions to a garden pool. They help the water feature reach and keep a good environmental balance. Koi, in particular, are known for their healthy appetite for water plants. However, if koi are purchased at the 4–5 inch size and not fed, they will peacefully coexist with plants while providing much viewing pleasure and entertainment.

Although ornamental fish will survive in a garden pool by eating insects and algae, most owners enjoy feeding them commercial pellets of fish food. Koi are quite trainable. They learn to come if you appear, clap your hands, or give some other sign on a regular basis just before feeding. Goldfish are slower to learn but they, too, can be taught to come at a signal if you have the patience to school them. Avoid overfeeding your fish.

ANIMALS (CONTINUED)

Once you have a garden pool or other water feature, you will soon discover that it appeals to a variety of native animals. Insects probably are among the first to discover a water feature. Mosquito larvae, appearing wherever water gathers in big and little pools, can be controlled with ornamental fish. Mayflies and caddisflies, two insects well-known to trout fishermen, are likely to frequent a garden pool, laying their eggs on the water surface. The larvae will grow up in the pond detritus. Dragonflies and damselflies are beautiful visitors to a water garden. They too may lay their eggs on the water, allowing the larvae to grow up in the pond bottom.

Amphibians, frogs, toads, and salamanders may discover the water almost as quickly as the insects. They are welcome visitors not only for their insectivorous appetites but also, in the case of frogs and toads, for their spring songs. They need easy ways to get in and out of the water. Small ramps or the equivalent will allow them easy access. The young tadpoles are vegetarian, feeding on pond algae and other plant material.

Snails often discover a water feature and adopt it as their home base. Freshwater shrimp and various kinds of water worms also may move into the garden pool. Microscopic water life is bound to appear too. You can discover organisms such as protozoa, hydra, and tiny alga with a home microscope.

Enjoy the diversity of your water garden. It's natural.

▼ Green frogs, bullfrogs, and others often become permanent residents of garden pools and ponds. They should be welcomed for the role they play in insect control.

GOLDFISH

Goldfish are related to small wild carp found in slow waters of southern China. Fish breeding programs going back as early as 265 AD have brought great variety of forms and colors that exist in goldfish today. Goldfish come in a stunning array of colors, patterns, and shapes.

When you bring fish home, float the bag in the garden pool for about 15 minutes to equalize the water temperatures. Open the bag and add some pond water to it. Float the bag another 15 minutes; then add more pond water. Repeat this once or twice, and then slide the fish into the pool water. New fish will be shy for a few days, but soon will become accustomed to you as you feed them. Feed no more than they will eat in one to two minutes.

For healthy fish, have no more than 2 inches of fish length (minus the tail) for each square foot of water surface. Cull excess fish. Check the pH and keep it between 7.0 and 8.0. Remove all dead plant material– decomposing plants and fish food are hazardous to the fish and the balance of the water. Keep an open place in winter ice or use a stock pond heater. Quarantine new fish for a week. Commercial water conditioner will make the water healthful for fish.

▶ **Goldfish come in many colors, types, and shapes that are good choices for garden pools.**

GOLDFISH

COMMON GOLDFISH

This is the fish we all remember from our earliest days, perhaps our first pet–one or two golden fish sitting in a small bowl on a table. Although the common goldfish remains small in its usually confined quarters, it will grow up to 9 inches in length in a larger pond or pool. The proportions of this hardy fish are even and it has a shallow fork in the tail. The highest point of the back is above the pectoral fins. This fish may be the usual gold, but silver, yellow, red, and even variegated variations occur.

COMET LONGTAIL GOLDFISH

The comets or comet longtails are very hardy goldfish that many experienced water gardeners believe are the finest fish for outdoor pools. They have long, flowing tails that in some cases are as long as their bodies. These fish breed easily. You may have to cull extra fish periodically to get the proper fish-to-water ratio. Comets will tolerate temperatures that are as low as 32°F or as high as 104°F.

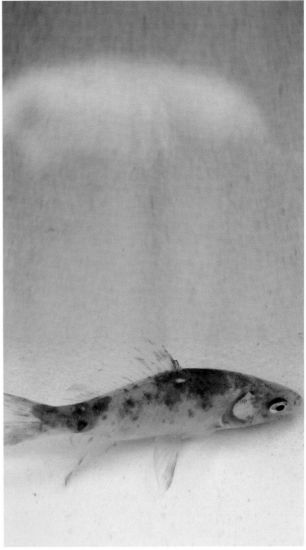

RED-AND-WHITE COMET

Comets come in many fancy color strains. Sarassas are red-and-white comets that have large red "caps" on their dorsal sides and white to silver over the rest of their bodies. Sarassa comets are not as hardy as common goldfish or comet longtails. They will thrive in a comparatively narrow temperature range of 46–68°F. For that reason, don't keep these fish in outdoor pools where summers are extremely hot or during winter months.

SHEBUNKIN

Shebunkins or calico fish appear almost scaleless but do have transparent scales. The name derives from the Japanese word that describes them as red with many other different colors, including blue, ochre, violet, and black. Shebunkins have single tails that may be short or long. They are good fish either for outdoor or indoor pools.

GOLDFISH

FANTAIL

Fantail goldfish have short egg-shape bodies and rarely grow more than 3–4 inches in length. The large tail, often appearing in profile as large as the body, is divided into three parts. Fantails may be as gold as the common goldfish, or red, red and white, or even several colors. The latter may be called calico fantails. Fantails must spend cold months indoors.

CHINESE MOOR

Moors are fantail goldfish of solid black. They have egg-shape bodies and three-part tails like the fantails. The eyes of moors may be just like the common goldfish or may be telescopic, that is, oddly swollen-looking eyes that protrude. Moors grow to about 4–5 inches in length. Take them indoors during the winter season as they are not very hardy.

ORANDA

Orandas are fancy goldfish with twin tails and hoods
or caps that look almost like raspberries. The caps are
prominent growths on the top of the head. The tails are
about ⅓ of the egg-shape body length. Orandas come
in a number of colors and color combinations, including
single-color gold or silver, red-cap, and calico. These
are less hardy than the common goldfish and should be
indoors during cold weather.

LIONHEAD

Lionheads have hoods, prominent growths that cover
much of the head, not just the crown. The tail fin is
divided and forked. In color, lionheads may be metallic
or calico. If metallic, the shiny metal colors extend into
the fins. If calico, they should have blue backgrounds with
patches of red, orange, yellow, purple, and brown, with
black spots. Like other fancy goldfish, the lionheads must
be indoors during the winter.

ORFES

GOLDEN ORFE

Because orfes might compete too successfully with native game fish, they are not allowed in some states with mild climates for fear that they might escape into natural waterways. Be sure to check state laws with your state department of conservation or natural resources before considering orfes for your water feature.

Orfes are fish for larger ponds and pools. They have, on occasion, jumped right out of smaller pools. They are lively, playful fish that are great for eating insects and mosquito larvae. Slender and almost bullet shape, the golden orfe will grow to a foot or more in length if it is in larger quarters. Orfes prefer to be with other fish so do not keep them singly. They may eat smaller fish but mix well with similar-size goldfish and koi. They are hardy and will spend cold weather somewhat dormant near the bottom of the pool.

Although they are more rare, especially in the United States, there are blue orfes as well as marbled types. The blue orfe is actually silver with dark blue on its back.

BLUE ORFE

OTHER FISH

GUPPY

Guppies *(Poecilla reticulata)* come in shapes and colors that range from plain to fancy. Tolerant of temperatures from 68–85°F, these natives of Central and South America bear live young and are omnivorous. Although they are short-lived (1-3 years), they are a good choice for a small pool. The 2½-inch-long females are a bit larger and rounder than the males. Keep two or more females per male. They readily breed, but since they are cannibalistic, provide fine-leafed foliage plants in the water to create hiding places for the young.

ROSY MINNOW

Some of the minnows, shiners, and darters of North American waters are suitable for garden pools in the summer, though if they are kept in small pools it would be wise to take them indoors during winter months. Although many of these small native American fish are rather dull in color, the rosy minnow *(Pimephales promelas)*, also called the fathead minnow, is a colorful addition to a garden feature. You can find them at most bait shops.

KOI

Koi, the colorful carp that are the national fish of Japan, are potentially large fish. Garden pools for koi ideally are deep (3–4 feet at the center) and at least 4×6 feet with steep sides. Koi pools are specialized for the care and display of these ornamental fish rather than for water plants. Koi eagerly eat water gardeners' prize lilies and other aquatic plants as well.

Koi specialists recommend that a good koi pond have a bottom drain, pump, and filter, a surface skimmer, and ultraviolet light. Yet, many people have had good success with koi in a multipurpose garden pool that does not have all of those technological advancements. Koi do have high oxygen demands and so the pool should have a waterfall or some other means for keeping it well-oxygenated.

Perhaps the best advice is to buy three or four small koi. Do not feed them. This causes them to lose their survival instinct, and encourages them to feed on plants. Avoid the temptation to add one big koi to the mix. A single large koi will feed on plants, and pass on bad habits to others.

◀ Koi come in many color combinations, some of which are valuable in the koi marketplace. They are easily trained to come to you to be fed.

Koi can be trained to come at a signal and to do such things as swim in a circle if you have the patience and are consistent in your training. Hungry animals are easy to train and koi are greedy feeders. The first thing to teach them is to come at a signal, a clap of the hands or tapping the water surface with a finger. Do that, then drop a couple of food pellets on the water. Continue until the fish come to the signal.

To teach them to go in a circle to the right, drop a food pellet any time the fish turns to the right. At the same time, move the hand with the food pellet to the right. Reward a right turn over a few days and soon the fish will begin turning to the right as you circle your hand to the right. Just as with dog training, make your signals clear and consistent, and the rewards small but worthwhile.

▲ **Even if you don't take the time to train your koi to come swimming up to you at a particular signal, they will reward you with their brilliant colors and playful antics in the water.**

The Japanese have established standards for koi based on the many color patterns that exist. There are single-color, metallic koi, and patterned koi. The following are among the more popular types of patterned koi. There also are other forms of koi, including butterfly koi and longfin koi. Choose small, young koi. They will grow fairly fast and, if in a good-size pool, may reach a foot or two, or even more, in length. Koi generally live 50 years, although there have been 100-year-old koi. While you may find that the fancy koi demand high prices, you often can find similarly marked fish at much lower prices in the collections of mixed koi that are in the marketplace.

KOHAKU KOI

This is the most popular of all the koi patterns. The Kohaku has a white body with a red accent pattern on the back. The red pattern may be pale red, crimson, a homogenous red, or a pattern with several shades of red. Further, the edge of the red pattern may be sharp or ragged. The shades of white, too, may be variable, coming in chalk white, eggshell, or yellowish white.

TAISHO SANKE KOI

Next in popularity is the Taisho Sanke koi. This tricolor koi has a white body with a red pattern on the back plus black accents. These fish are like the ever-popular Kohaku described at left but with black markings in addition. Some of these black markings are large and some small. As the fish age, the black markings may begin to look cracked or may even break up into many pieces.

SHOWA SANSHOKU KOI

The Showa Sanke or Showa Sanshoku is the third most popular type of koi. This tricolor koi has a black body with red and white accents. These fish are almost all black when they first hatch, but within a few days, white patterns begin to show up against the black background. Eventually red patterns develop on top of the white patterns. The insides of their mouths remain black throughout their entire lives.

UTSURIMONO KOI

This bicolor koi is the Utsuri or Utsurimono. This fish has black skin and markings of white, red, or yellow. Its pectoral fins are striped. Koi fanciers divide this category of koi into three sections, depending upon whether the interlaced markings are white, red, or yellow.

NATIVE FISH

Some of the popular baitfish that are farm-raised or hand-netted by fishermen will be good fish for water garden pools and ponds. They may not be as bright and flashy as goldfish or koi, but they are natives and might be excellent choices for those who like to grow native plants in their water gardens. These fish are great for insect control, including mosquitoes.

To get them for your garden pool or container water garden, visit a local bait store or take a hand seine to an area stream. The fish you might find in either location would be worth trying out in your water feature. As natives, you know they will tolerate local temperatures. If they are from swiftly flowing streams, this probably means that they thrive on high levels of oxygen. They would be healthier in a pool with a fountain or waterfall to aerate the water.

◄ Bluegills are named for the characteristic deep blue color of their gills. These small native fish adapt to water gardens better than some other native fish. Stock them in your pond, and they'll delight you with their antics.

RAINBOW DACE

(Notropis lutrensis). These small fish are long and thin.
Dace are good for mosquito control. They are bright and
striking-looking when they are in the sunlight. They are
native to cool waters and cannot tolerate warm to hot
water. The rainbow dace grows 2–3 inches in length.

GOLDEN SHINER

(Notemigonus crysoleucas). These fish are native or introduced
throughout much of the continental United States. They
are thin but deep-bodied with sides of silver or gold. From
above, they look greenish brown. Their mouths turn up
and the tails are deeply forked. They have been popular
baitfish since the 1940s. Shiners will eat a wide variety of
natural foods from insects and plankton to algae. They
also will eat manufactured fish foods. Golden shiners
grow up to 6 inches in length.

OTHER ANIMALS

Garden pools and ponds attract many different animals both good and bad, plus some with mixed reviews depending on the situation. Unless you are in the deepest heart of a major metropolitan area, your garden pool will probably attract a variety of insects, mammals, amphibians, birds, and reptiles.

Frogs and toads like to hang around water for a number of reasons. Water attracts many insects that are food for these amphibians. Accessible water also is the breeding place of toads and frogs. In the spring, you are likely to have tadpoles added to your mix of plants and fish. In the spring, frogs and toads sing during the early breeding season providing one of nature's favorite symphonies.

Birds also are attracted to water. They, too, find the insect life tasty and abundant. They need water to drink in an accessible place. This is especially important during droughty summer spells. Some birds are attracted to water because they eat fish.

▲ Frogs are among the most common visitors to water gardens. If you have native frogs nearby, they almost certainly will take up residence in your water garden.

► Turtles, such as these painted turtles, may find their way to your garden pond.

Turtles may find their way into your garden pool. Some of them travel overland considerable distances in search of new waters to conquer. While painted turtles and some of the other natives would be welcome additions, snapping turtles might be hazardous to the health of fish and even of the water gardener.

Native water snails sometimes find their way into garden pools and ponds. They are algae eaters for the most part and so will be welcome additions to the pool.

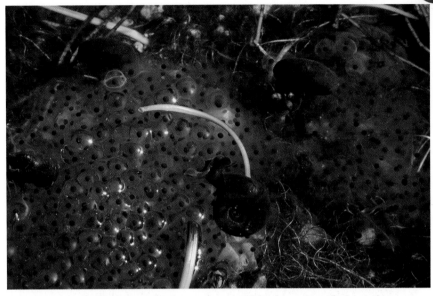

▲ Frogs may lay their eggs in the pool or pond in the spring. Their mating songs signal the arrival of spring. Watching tadpoles mature and morph into frogs is a fascinating process.

▲ Raccoons also may find their way to your water feature. They are not welcome as they enjoy a diet that includes fish, including your fancy koi.

If raccoons, blue herons, and other animals are feeding on your fish, the best way to repel them is to get a motion-triggered water spray and carefully aim it at the places where the animals or birds like to fish. This is a fairly recent innovation in the pest-control field. Other ways to keep animals out are fences that, depending on the animals, must be tall and designed to keep out such creatures as raccoons and deer. A low-voltage electric fence can be a powerful deterrent to some animals, including deer, raccoons, and local pets. There also are repellents that smell or taste bad. Netting placed over the surface of a garden pool will dissuade herons from fishing there. Live-trapping and transporting animals is not very successful in most cases because other animals will move into the territory.

Another solution, an odd but successful one that might be used against such pests as raccoons, would be making a moat of black plastic around the garden. Animals don't like to walk on the material. To further pest-proof it, sprinkle some hydrated lime powder, the kind used to make lines on athletic fields, on the plastic moat. Animals, especially raccoons, don't

▶ Great blue herons raise havoc in a koi pool and can gulp through a school of goldfish in no time.

▼ Domestic cats are often unwelcome visitors to water gardens as they enjoy an occasional treat of fish.

This great egret is beautiful to watch but he is a skilled fisher, and can catch fish as fast as you add them to the pool.

like to get that powder on their feet. They have to lick it off and it is distasteful.

Fences are good pest-prevention methods for domestic dogs, cats, and, not the least of potential garden pool pests, neighborhood children. As far as children are concerned, local ordinances may require fences for garden pools over a certain depth and/or size. Be sure to check with authorities.

All in all, the majority of the animals that find their way into your water garden are harmless and make good additions to the garden. Enjoy them and figure out easy ways to discourage those animals that are less welcome.

▲ Mallard ducks eat insects and plant matter, so you need not fear losing your prize fish to their predation.

WATER GARDENING SOURCES

When buying water gardening plants and supplies, support your local nurseries and suppliers. If you can't find what you want in the local marketplace, check with one of these mail-order firms. Water gardening societies can be another good source of information.

Al Zimmer Ponds & Supplies

6271 Perkiomen Ave.

Birdsboro, PA 19508

800/722-8877

www.azponds.com

Aqua-Mart, Inc.

P.O. Box 547399

Orlando, FL 32854-7399

800/245-5814

www.aqua-mart.com

Aquascape Designs, Inc.

St. Charles, IL 60174

www.aquascapedesigns.com

Aquatic Pond Supplies

494 S. Court St.

Crown Point, IN 46307

219/662-9596

www.aquaticpondsupplies.com

Associated Koi Clubs of America

P.O. Box 1

Midway City, CA 92655

800/660-2073

www.akca.org

Beckett Water Gardening

5931 Campus Circle Dr.

Irving, TX 75063-2606

888/BECKETT

www.888beckett.com

Drs. Foster and Smith

2253 Air Park Rd.

Rhinelander, WI 54501

800/381-7179

www.drsfostersmith.com

International Waterlily and Water Gardening Society

6828 26th St. W

Bradenton, FL 34207

941/756-0880

www.iwgs.org

Lilyblooms Aquatic Gardens

932 S. Main St.

North Canton, OH 44720

800/921-0005

www.lilyblooms.com

Lilypons Water Gardens

6800 Lilypons Rd., Box 10

Adamstown, MD 21710

800/999-5459

www.lilypons.com

M & S Ponds and Supplies

12635 Danielson Ct. #202

Poway, CA 92064

858/679-8729

www.msponds.com

Maryland Aquatic Nurseries, Inc.

3427 N Furnace Rd.

Jarrettsville, MD 21084

410/557-7615

www.marylandaquatic.com

Paradise Water Gardens, Ltd.

14 May St.

Whitman, MA 02382

800/955-0161

www.paradisewatergardens.com

Perry's Water Gardens

136 Gibson Aquatic Farm Rd.

Franklin, NC 28734

828/524-3264

perrywat@dnet.net

Pond-A-Rama

9858 McCreary Rd.

Shippensburg, PA 17257

717/532-7212

www.pondarama.com

Slocum Water Gardens

P.O. Box 7079

Winter Haven, FL 33884

863/293-7151

www.slocumwatergardens.com

Suburban Water Gardens, Inc.

211 Burrs Ave.

Dix Hills, NY 11746

631/643-3500

www.suburbanpond.com

Van Ness Water Gardens

2460 North Euclid Ave.

Upland, CA 91784

800/205-2425

www.vnwg.com

William Tricker, Inc.

7125 Tanglewood Dr.

Independence, OH 44131

800/524-3492

www.tricker.com

WEBSITES

www.aquatic-gardeners.org

Aquatic Gardeners Association. International association offering information, quarterly journal, meetings.

www.pondplants.com

Source for freshwater plants.

www.thekrib.com

Tropical fish.

www.theplantplace.com

Unusual plants for water gardens.

GLOSSARY

Acidity—A pH value of less than 7.0.

Aerate—To supply air to the water in a pond or pool. Aeration helps prevent oxygen depletion and water stagnation.

Algae—Plantlike organisms that grow in ponds and streams. Some algae are beneficial while others, such as floating phytoplankton and green string algae, are not. Abundant algae turn the water murky green. Development is more rapid in warm, well-lit water.

Alkalinity—A pH value of more than 7.0.

Annual—A plant that lives for one growing season, then dies. An annual must be replanted each spring unless it naturally sows its seeds and resprouts from the seeds the following spring.

Aquatic plant—Any plant that can grow and thrive with its roots in water or in water-saturated soil.

Barbel—A soft threadlike appendage near the mouth of some fish including koi. Fish species may be identified by the number, shape, and placement of barbels.

Biennial—Any plant that grows vegetatively its first year, and flowers and dies during the second growing season after it germinates.

Biota—The combined plant and animal life of an environment.

Bog garden—A garden with soil that is permanently damp to wet.

Bog plant—A plant that will grow and prosper with its roots in wet soil.

Boulder—A large stone, often round or egg-shape, weathered and worn fairly smooth.

Bowl fountain—A water feature with one or more bowls, usually on a central stem. Water, which sometimes sprays into the air from the top, spills from one bowl to the next, and often pours into a pool beneath the fountain.

Butyl—The rubber material that is used as a strong and durable waterproof liner for ponds, pools, and other water features.

Carpenter's level—A tool for checking whether an item is perfectly horizontal or vertical.

Chloramine—A chemical added to water to kill harmful organisms in it. Chloramine must be removed for healthy plant and animal growth.

Circuit breaker—An automatic switch that cuts electrical power if a short circuit or a power overload exceeds the preset safety level.

Cultivar—A cultivated variety that represents a plant variation within a species that has originated in cultivation.

Cutting—The part of a plant (bud, leaf, stem, or root) that is removed and used to asexually propagate the plant.

Deadheading—The act of removing spent flowers to encourage additional bloom and to improve the plant's appearance.

Deciduous—A plant that sheds its leaves at the end of the growing season and grows new ones at the beginning of the next growing season.

Dormancy—A condition that usually occurs during winter when plant growth temporarily shuts down.

Ecology—The study of the relationships of plants and animals with their environments and with each other.

Ecosystem—A biological community of interacting plants and animals in their physical environment.

EPDM—Ethylene propylene diene monomer. A type of pond liner material.

Evergreen—A plant that holds its leaves or needles through more than one growing season.

Flexible liner—Waterproof EPDM, vinyl, or other plastic material used to line water features.

Flow adjuster—A valve that is adjustable and controls the flow of water.

Genus—The classification group that falls between family and species. Includes a group of closely related species.

Geotextile—A nonwoven fabric underlay used under mulch in landscaping or under a liner in a water garden.

Grade—(noun) The level of the ground at a project. (verb) To change, level, or smooth the surface of the ground.

Gravel—Small, loose rocks. Natural gravel, with pebbles that are smooth and rounded, often comes from rivers. Crushed gravel, with irregular, jagged pebbles, comes from larger rocks that are mechanically crushed.

Ground fault circuit interrupter (GFCI)—A device that shuts off electrical power to an electrical device the moment it senses that water has come in contact with bare wiring. Also may be called ground fault interrupter (GFI).

Hybrid—A plant that results from crossing of two different species, varieties, or lines.

Indigenous—A plant or animal native to a specific region.

Inorganic fertilizer—A manufactured product used to improve soil fertility. Most contain nitrogen, phosphorus, potassium, or a combination of these three elements.

Invasive—A plant that spreads far beyond its planned site.

Landscape fabric—A nonwoven fabric that allows water and air to pass through but blocks weed growth.

Marginal plant—A plant that grows and thrives in shallow water or moist to wet soil at the edge of a water feature.

Marginal shelf—A shallow shelf created in a pool or pond expressly for marginal plants.

Marsh—A wet zone that is partially or totally flooded and rich in plant life.

Native plant—A plant that originates from the country or region in which it is being grown.

Naturalized—A plant that grows and reproduces on its own in a region where it is not native.

Neutral—A pH value of 7.0.

One-way valve—A valve that allows water to flow only in one direction.

Organic fertilizer—A substance derived from decomposed plant or animal material, or a naturally occurring mineral, used to improve soil fertility.

Oxygenator—A plant that grows underwater and releases oxygen into the water as a byproduct of photosynthesis. Also referred to as a submerged plant.

Paver—A stone or cast-concrete piece used in constructing paths and patios.

Perennial—A plant that lives for several or many years. It need not be replanted every year. It may take several years to mature.

pH—A measure of acidity or alkalinity.

Photosynthesis—The process by which green plants produce carbohydrates and oxygen from carbon dioxide and water in the presence of light energy.

Plumb line—A string with a metal weight that is used to determine a true vertical dimension.

Polyethylene—An inexpensive, flexible, and waterproof pond liner used for low-cost installations.

Pond liner—Flexible rubber or plastic sheeting or rigid fiberglass or resin placed in a pond excavation to prevent water from draining through the soil.

Preformed unit—A ready-made rigid form used for garden pools and streams.

Propagation—The process of increasing plants by sexual (seed) means or asexual (vegetative) means.

PVC—Short for polyvinyl chloride, a durable and waterproof material.

Sedge—A grasslike plant with triangular stems that usually grows in damp to wet areas.

Spadix—The thick, fleshy spike or club in certain kinds of flowers; often surrounded by a spathe.

Spathe—A conspicuous bract or modified leaf that surrounds a spadix in certain flowers.

Spawning—The reproductive activity and period in fish.

Species—A category of classification of organisms that are more similar to one another than a genus, but differ more from one another than a variety or cultivar.

Stepping-stone—A flat stone large enough for a footstep; used to construct a path.

Stolon—A prostrate stem that grows along the surface of or just below the ground surface.

Submerged plant—A plant that grows underwater; often called an oxygenator because it releases oxygen into the water as a byproduct of photosynthesis.

Submersible pump—A pump that is housed and runs underwater.

Surface pump—A pump that is housed and runs on dry land.

Transformer—A device for reducing or increasing the voltage of electrical current.

Turbid—Water that is cloudy because of suspended particles of solid matter.

Underlayment—A nonwoven synthetic fabric placed under a pond liner to prevent punctures and tears to the liner.

UV—Ultraviolet. Light rays with wavelengths that fall between the violet end of the spectrum and X-rays.

Water table—The level of soil water in an area below which water will not drain away.

Wick effect—The tendency of water to move from a pool into surrounding soil as it follows plant roots or some materials.

USDA PLANT HARDINESS ZONE MAP

This map of climate zones helps you select plants for your garden that will survive a typical winter in your region. The United States Department of Agriculture (USDA) developed the map, basing the zones on the lowest recorded temperatures across North America. Zone 1 is the coldest area and Zone 11 is the warmest.

Plants are classified by the coldest temperature and zone they can endure. For example, plants hardy to Zone 6 survive where winter temperatures drop to –10° F. Those hardy to Zone 8 die long before it's that cold. These plants may grow in colder regions but must be replaced each year. Plants rated for a range of hardiness zones can usually survive winter in the coldest region as well as tolerate the summer heat of the warmest one.

To find your hardiness zone, note the approximate location of your community on the map, then match the color band marking that area to the key.

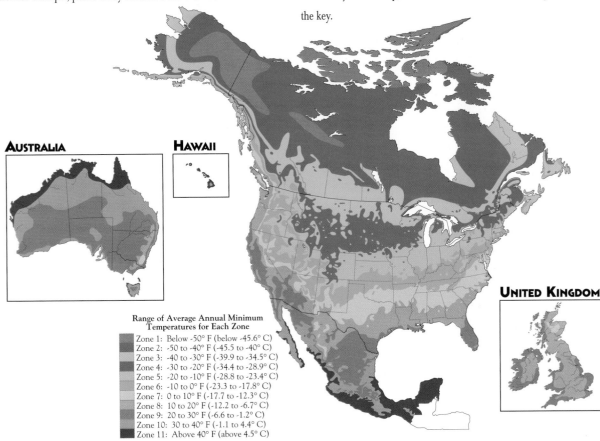

AUSTRALIA

HAWAII

UNITED KINGDOM

Range of Average Annual Minimum Temperatures for Each Zone

- Zone 1: Below -50° F (below -45.6° C)
- Zone 2: -50 to -40° F (-45.5 to -40° C)
- Zone 3: -40 to -30° F (-39.9 to -34.5° C)
- Zone 4: -30 to -20° F (-34.4 to -28.9° C)
- Zone 5: -20 to -10° F (-28.8 to -23.4° C)
- Zone 6: -10 to 0° F (-23.3 to -17.8° C)
- Zone 7: 0 to 10° F (-17.7 to -12.3° C)
- Zone 8: 10 to 20° F (-12.2 to -6.7° C)
- Zone 9: 20 to 30° F (-6.6 to -1.2° C)
- Zone 10: 30 to 40° F (-1.1 to 4.4° C)
- Zone 11: Above 40° F (above 4.5° C)

METRIC CONVERSIONS

U.S. UNITS TO METRIC EQUIVALENTS			METRIC UNITS TO U.S. EQUIVALENTS		
TO CONVERT FROM	MULTIPLY BY	TO GET	TO CONVERT FROM	MULTIPLY BY	TO GET
Inches	25.4	Millimeters	Millimeters	0.0394	Inches
Inches	2.54	Centimeters	Centimeters	0.3937	Inches
Feet	30.48	Centimeters	Centimeters	0.0328	Feet
Feet	0.3048	Meters	Meters	3.2808	Feet
Yards	0.9144	Meters	Meters	1.0936	Yards

To convert from degrees Fahrenheit (F) to degrees Celsius (C), first subtract 32, then multiply by 5/9.

To convert from degrees Celsius to degrees Fahrenheit, multiply by 9/5, then add 32.

Spring and Autumn Frost Dates

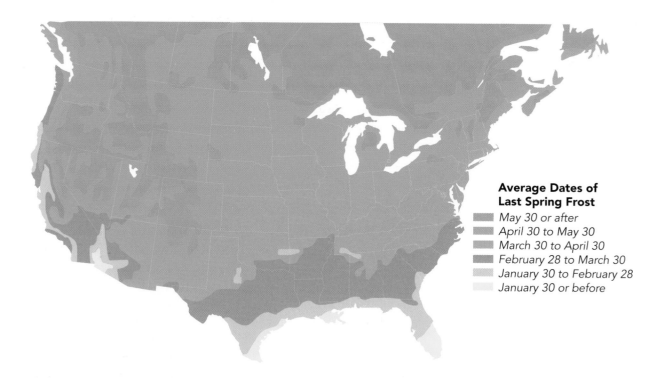

**Average Dates of
Last Spring Frost**

- May 30 or after
- April 30 to May 30
- March 30 to April 30
- February 28 to March 30
- January 30 to February 28
- January 30 or before

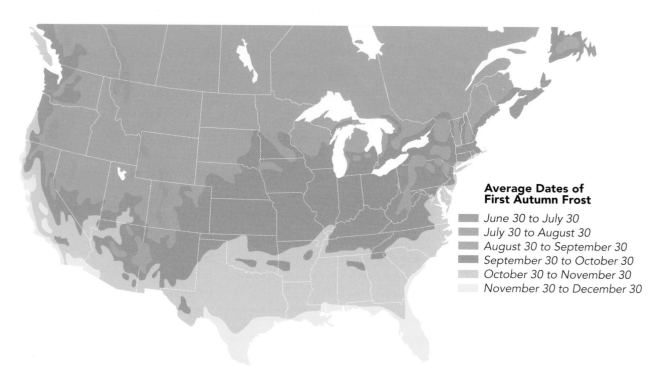

**Average Dates of
First Autumn Frost**

- June 30 to July 30
- July 30 to August 30
- August 30 to September 30
- September 30 to October 30
- October 30 to November 30
- November 30 to December 30

INDEX

Page numbers in **bold** type indicate main descriptions of topics and include photographs. Page numbers in *italic* type indicate additional photographs. All plants and animals are listed under their common names.

ORTHO®

watergardens
tranquility+beauty

ORTHO® **ALL ABOUT BUILDING**

Waterfalls,
Ponds, and Streams

ALL NEW EDITION

Creating
Water Gardens
ORTHO®

BUILDING ■ GROWING ■ HOW-TO

ORTHO® **ALL ABOUT**

Garden Pools
& Fountains
ALL NEW EDITION

expertadvice

inspiration+ideas+how-to
for designing, building, maintaining